GOING BANANAS

WITH DEMENTIA

David Lloyd Strauss

Print ISBN: 979-8-9857860-7-1
eBook ISBN: 979-8-9857860-8-8

First edition

Version 11.01.2024 | November 2024

SERIES: Going Bananas

Published by: Giggle Yoga LLC

PO Box 28

Boulder, CO 80306

All images created with Dalle

Cover Design: Spare Design | Barbara Wade

Ouray, Colorado

Book Production: Book Your Brand LLC

This book is dedicated to my dad, Arthur Michel Strauss, who taught me the true meaning of patience, love, and humor—even in the toughest of times. Your laughter, endless stories, yodeling, and love for bananas will always be cherished. This book is for you and for every moment we shared, knowing that your spirit and joy will continue to live on every page.

March 19th, 1926 — August 27th, 2020

3

Contents

DEAR FRIEND...

May this book offer you the wisdom, patience, humor, and grace you need as you care for your loved one. I know firsthand how challenging and emotional this journey can be, but I also know how full of love and meaning it is. My hope is that through these pages, you'll find moments of comfort, connection, and maybe even a little laughter to help you through the tough times.

Caring for someone with memory loss is no small task. It requires more than just physical care—it calls for an open heart, a lot of patience, and a willingness to embrace the unexpected. There will be days when it's overwhelming, but there will also be days when you share small, joyful moments that remind you why this journey is so important.

I hope this book serves as a reminder that you're not alone. Others have walked this path, and we've all learned that sometimes, in the smallest moments, you find the deepest connection. May this book bring you encouragement, a sense of peace, and a little inspiration to keep going, even on the hardest days.

You're doing an incredible job, and I hope this book helps lighten the load just a bit, guiding you with love and warmth.

With heartfelt support!

BIG LOVE,

David Strauss

CAN A BANANA CHANGE YOUR LIFE?

Here's a question for you:

Have you ever thought a banana could change your life? Sounds strange, right? I didn't either—until I became a caregiver for my dad, who had dementia. That's when I learned that sometimes the simplest things—like a banana—can make all the difference when life feels completely upside down. My dad may be gone now, but the lessons we learned together, the laughter we shared, and, yep, even the tears during those difficult and uncomfortable moments are all still with me. And now, I want to pass those on to you.

This book isn't about giving you a step-by-step guide to caregiving—it's about helping you find joy in the unexpected, learning to let go of the things you can't control, and embracing the moments that make you laugh, even when life feels hard. I've learned that in caregiving, it's not just about the practical stuff—it's about finding ways to navigate the emotional twists and turns and maybe, just maybe, laughing when things get a little weird. After all, if we can't find some humor in this journey, what are we doing?

Caring for someone with dementia is heartwarming one minute, exhausting the next, and somehow, in the middle of all the confusion, you'll find moments that are just downright funny. Yep, funny—because if there's one thing I picked up along the way, it's that humor is your best friend, helping you to make it through the many emotional gyrations of memory care. Whether it's hearing the same story for the 12th time with just as much excitement as the first or watching them peel a banana like it's the best thing ever, those little moments will remind you what really matters.

But here's the thing: caregiving isn't just about the hard parts. It's filled with moments of love and connection that will stay with you forever. And if I could get through it—armed with bananas, a sense of humor, and a whole lot of love—I know you can, too.

So, welcome to the banana-filled world of caregiving! It's messy, unpredictable, and sometimes downright overwhelming, but it's also full of love, connection, and moments that will stay with you forever. Together, let's peel back the layers and dive into this wild, love-filled ride. You're not alone—and if you need a break, well, there's always a banana waiting.

THANKS FOR THE BANANA!

My dad loved bananas—not just casually—he adored them. Throughout his life, bananas were his go-to snack, his little yellow slice of happiness. So, when dementia started creeping into his world, and he moved into memory care, I knew exactly what to bring him on my visits: bananas.

I'll never forget the day I showed up with a bunch of bananas. The moment he saw them, his face lit up like it was Christmas morning. "Wow, you brought me bananas!" he said, his eyes wide with excitement, as if he was seeing a banana for the very first time.

"Sure did, Dad," I said, handing him one. He peeled it with the same enthusiasm I'd seen a thousand times, took a bite, and savored it like it was the best thing he'd ever tasted. We sat there, chatting and laughing, and a few minutes later, without missing a beat, he looked at me again, all excited, and said, "Wow, you brought me bananas! Can I have one?"

I had to laugh. "Of course, Dad," I said, handing him another. And, just like that, we were back at square one. He peeled it, took a bite, and enjoyed it with the same childlike wonder. This happened again and again. Every few minutes, he'd rediscover those bananas with the same delight. By the end of our visit, he'd eaten seven bananas—each one bringing him as much joy as the first.

That's the thing about dementia. My dad may have forgotten he'd already eaten a banana, but the joy he felt every time was real. And that day, I realized something important: sometimes, you've just got to let go and go bananas with them.

Those banana moments became more than just quirky stories to laugh about later—they were lessons. I learned that caregiving wasn't about correcting my dad or reminding him he'd already eaten a banana. It wasn't about controlling the situation. It was about being there, in the moment, and sharing in his joy, even if it meant handing him another banana for the 7th time.

Caregiving for someone with dementia isn't always easy. There are days when the repetition can drive you a little crazy—hearing the same question or story over and over. But those banana moments taught me to look beyond the frustration and see the joy. Each time he lit up over a banana, it was a reminder that, despite the memory loss, there were still moments of pure, unfiltered happiness.

During those final five years, bananas became our little ritual. I'd bring a bunch on every visit, knowing my dad would be just as thrilled with the seventh banana as he was with the first. It wasn't about the snack itself—it was about creating a moment of connection. That's what caregiving became for me: finding those small, simple ways to connect, even if it was just through a piece of fruit.

Looking back, those bananas were about more than just feeding my dad. They were about love, patience, and learning to be present. Caregiving isn't just about the practical stuff—it's about finding joy in the little things. Handing my dad another banana wasn't frustrating; it was a way to create happiness over and over again. It was a chance to

let go of expectations and just *be* with him, wherever he was at that moment.

So, when I think of caregiving, I think of bananas—not because they were his favorite, but because they taught me to embrace the present, find joy in the simplest things, and connect in ways that didn't need words or memories. Those small, repeated acts of love are what made the journey worthwhile.

The pages that follow are the lessons I learned from caring for my dad. They're about finding humor in the repetition, embracing the quiet moments, and realizing that caregiving isn't just about helping someone live—it's about helping them live with dignity and joy. Yes, there were many difficult times, but for me, I want to help others magnify the magical moments. So, grab a banana (or whatever brings your loved one joy), and let's walk through this journey together.

Part One
Helpful Tips

Helpful Tip # 1
Bananas Are Always a Good Idea

If you're caring for someone with dementia, you know it's the familiar things that bring them the most joy. For my dad, it was a simple, sweet treat that made his face light up on every occasion. Over time, I realized that bananas weren't just his favorite snack; they became a kind of metaphor for the things that make someone with dementia feel comforted and happy. Your loved one might have their own "banana"—maybe it's the sound of a familiar tune, the softness of a favorite blanket, playing cards, or the feel of the sun on their skin. The trick is figuring out what that "banana" is for them and letting them have it as often as they want.

I remember a charming grandmother who lived in my dad's memory care home. She loved knitting. Even with her faded memory, her hands still remembered how to knit. Every time she picked up those needles,

it was like she found a little bit of peace. It wasn't about whether she finished the scarf or hat she started—it was just about the joy she felt in the process. That's the key: finding what brings them peace and what makes them feel connected with themselves, whether it's a ball of yarn or their military veteran hat that gives them a sense of pride—and letting them enjoy it.

Their "banana" may be sitting in a favorite chair or flipping through an old photo album, reliving memories—even if they're doing it for the hundredth time. Whatever it is, you'll start to see how much these little routines bring comfort and connection.

I knew another family whose father loved sitting in his garden. He couldn't remember the names of the flowers or even recognize some of the people visiting him, but the moment he felt the sun on his face, he was at peace. Those moments in the garden became his way of feeling calm and connected.

It's important to let your loved one have those small joys, whatever form they take. Look at it through their eyes. For people with dementia, everyone is a stranger. They may remember a few family members or close friends, but those folks are not always around, so anything that makes them feel at home is soothing for them. I remember a woman who told me that whenever her mother held her favorite soft blanket, she would instantly calm down. It didn't matter why the blanket worked—it just made her feel safe and secure.

Another friend found that her husband, who loved opera, would still hum along to his favorite songs even when most of his memory had slipped away. She'd play those arias again and again, and he would close his eyes and hum softly as if the music took him somewhere familiar. That music was his way of finding joy in the moment.

So, think of "bananas" as more than just food—think of them as the little things that make your loved one feel alive and connected, and that's what truly matters.

Helpful Tip # 2
Go Bananas! Embrace the Repetition.

When you're caring for someone with dementia, the repetition can be exhausting. The same questions, the same stories, the same routine—over and over, day in and day out. I know firsthand how draining it can feel. There were days when I thought, "Here we go again," as the same story unfolded for the fifth time in an hour. But then, one day, I realized something that shifted everything for me: for my dad, it wasn't the same old story. For him, each time he shared a memory or rediscovered something he loved, it was like pressing reset on a moment of happiness.

The trick to embracing repetition is to lean into it, to treat it as a chance to be present with your loved one, even if you've heard it all before. Every time my dad told me how much he loved bananas or repeated one of his favorite stories from his vast repertoire, I could have easily reminded him that he had just told me or just eaten one. But instead, I handed him another banana and let him enjoy it like it was the first time. The repetition wasn't the point—it was the happiness in his eyes, the joy of that moment, and being with him fully as he relived it. That's what mattered most.

One thing I learned through this journey is that repetition isn't just a symptom of dementia—it's a way of creating comfort and familiarity, both for you and your loved one. Even if you've heard the same story or answered the same question a dozen times, for them, it's fresh every time. They're not just repeating the words—they're reliving the emotions tied to that moment.

Instead of focusing on the fact that you've heard the story before, try focusing on the joy your loved one feels as they tell it again—it's about their joy. Watch how their face lights up when they talk about a favorite memory or when they ask you about something they love. Repetition can be exhausting, but it can also be a gift—it's a way to tap into their joy and create a connection that goes beyond words. Use it as an opportunity for your own self-reflection. What joyful memories do you have that are worth repeating?

For my dad, every time he ate a banana, it was like tasting it for the first time. The delight he found in that simple act became something I looked forward to. I stopped seeing it as "here we go again" and started seeing it as an opportunity to share in his happiness, over and over.

One of the ways I found peace in the repetition was by turning it into a ritual. It became something to look forward to, something that brought us both comfort. For me and my dad, it was our banana conversations. Every visit, we'd go through the same dialogue about how much he loved bananas, and it became a little tradition of ours—one that made both of us smile.

Maybe your loved one has a favorite story they love to tell. Instead of getting tired of hearing it, try leaning into it. Ask questions, even if you already know the answers. The goal isn't to hear something new—it's to connect with them through something they cherish. It's not about the story itself; it's about creating a moment that's meaningful to them.

With my dad, I embraced what I now call the "bananas-on-repeat" philosophy. It wasn't about counting how many bananas he ate or how many times we had the same conversation. It was about being present with him in each moment as if it were brand new. I stopped keeping track of the repetition and started counting the smiles instead. And honestly, those smiles were worth everything.

Repetition became a gift. It gave us more opportunities to share joy, relive happy memories, and connect over something familiar. Dementia may take away the ability to create new memories, but it gives us the chance to savor the moments that remain—again and again. Each retelling, each repeated question, became a chance to be fully present with him, and that's where the magic lies.

When the Loop Becomes Love

Here's the real truth I discovered: the loop of repetition isn't just a symptom of dementia—it's a form of love. Each time your loved one repeats the same story or asks the same question, they're reaching out to you, inviting you into their world. It's their way of connecting, and it's up to us to meet them where they are.

When that familiar loop starts again—whether it's about a favorite snack, a cherished memory, or just a simple question—embrace it. Play along, smile, and engage as if it's the first time. For them, it *is* the first time. And in that space, you'll find something deeper—a connection that's built on love, trust, and shared joy. Repetition becomes a way to keep that connection alive, no matter how many times the story is told.

In the end, it's not about trying to create new memories or escape the cycle of repetition. It's about leaning into the joy that still exists, even if it's the same moment on repeat. That's the power of forgetting—it gives you and your loved one a fresh start every five minutes. And in that fresh start, you'll find a love that's worth celebrating over and over again. They will die soon enough, so cherish and learn from the simplicity of their condition.

Helpful Tip # 3
Laughter & Giggles. The Best Medicine.

Humor is your best friend when caring for someone with dementia, and I mean *really* your best friend. Think of it as your secret weapon—like a banana peel you can slip on without falling, just to lighten up the moment. Dementia brings enough serious moments, so when you find those pockets of humor, grab onto them and never let go. Laughter has this magic ability to break through the fog, even if it's just for a second, and in that moment, it feels like everything is okay.

My dad loved silly jokes, and even as his memory started to slip, he could still crack up at the simplest punchlines. One day, I brought a book of knock-knock jokes, and we spent an hour just going through them. Each one was a hit—even though I'm pretty sure I told him the same jokes at least three times in a row.

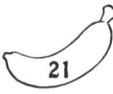

21

> *"Knock knock." "Who's there?" "Banana." "Banana who?"*
> *"Banana split, let's get out of here!"*
> *"Knock knock." "Who's there?" "Banana." "Banana who?"*
> *"Banana split, let's slip into something fun!"*
> *"Knock knock." "Who's there?" "Orange." "Orange who?"*
> *"Orange you glad I didn't say banana?"*

He'd laugh like he'd never heard it before. The punchline wasn't even the point—it was the joy of the exchange. And let's be honest, who doesn't love a good knock-knock joke?

So, here's a tip: find what makes your loved one laugh and *lean into* it. Whether it's knock-knock jokes, old puns, or silly observations, let humor fill the space where words sometimes fail.

The Accidental Comedy Show

One thing dementia brings along is unintentional comedy. There was this one time I visited my dad, and we were having lunch. Out of nowhere, he looked at his plate and said, "Who invited these potatoes? They're not on the guest list!" Now, where that came from, I have no idea—but we both started laughing. It became our little running gag. Anytime we had a meal together, we'd "check the guest list" to see if any of the food items were invited. He may not have remembered the joke from the previous day, but at that moment, we had a connection through laughter.

Another time, he asked me for ketchup, but when I handed him the bottle, he started pouring it directly onto his napkin. I couldn't help but laugh, and when he realized what he'd done, he laughed too. Dementia may steal a lot, but it doesn't steal the ability to find joy in absurd moments. And let's be real—sometimes, it's the little mishaps that become the best memories.

Humor doesn't have to be random—it can be a part of your daily interactions. Try making up a few recurring jokes that you both share. For example, you could have a running joke about their favorite TV show or create a funny nickname for their favorite chair. In my dad's case, he started calling his walker "The Hot Rod." He even had a horn on it. Every time we went for a walk, I'd say, "Okay, Dad, let's take the Hot Rod out for a spin!" and he'd respond with, "Let's burn some

rubber!" It made the daily routine a bit more fun, and it gave him a sense of control, even when everything else felt out of reach.

Can You Get Them to Giggle? Here's a game you can try with your loved one: see how many times you can make them laugh in a single visit. Whether it's through silly jokes, funny faces, or even just playing with words, aim to collect as many giggles as you can. I used to challenge myself to get my dad to laugh at least five times before I left. Sometimes, I'd even make it into a playful competition: "Alright, Dad, I'm going for the record today—five laughs before I leave!" It gave us both something to look forward to and on the harder days, it reminded me to find the lightness in the situation.

Humor as a Lifeline in Tough Times

There are going to be tough moments when things get frustrating or sad. That's when humor can be your lifeline. When my dad would get upset because he couldn't remember something, I'd try to lighten the mood with a joke or a silly comment. One time, he got frustrated trying to put on his jacket, so I said, "Looks like that jacket's playing hard to get, huh?" He paused, looked at me, and then we both laughed. That little break in the tension helped him relax, and we were able to move forward. In those hard moments, it's okay to laugh *with* them, not *at* them. Humor can be a gentle way to pull them out of a difficult emotional space and bring them back to something lighter.

Here's the best part: the punchline doesn't matter. Whether it's a well-timed joke or just a funny face, the point is the connection you create in that moment. Dementia might take away memory, but it can't take away laughter. So, embrace the humor wherever you find it. Whether you're telling the same knock-knock joke three times or playing a silly game of "Where did I put my glasses," the joy of the moment is what counts.

Humor lightens the load, creates moments of joy, and helps you both find a connection in the midst of it all. When words and memories fade, laughter is a language that always speaks loud and clear.

Helpful Tip # 4
Riding the Roller Coaster 'Wait, What Was I Saying?'

With dementia, conversations can feel like you've hopped onto a roller coaster with a banana peel under your feet—one minute, you're talking about lunch, and the next, you're halfway through a story about their childhood, only to slip mid-sentence and end up somewhere entirely different. It's a ride that might seem a bit dizzying at times, with unexpected twists, turns, and sudden stops. But here's the thing: this roller coaster is worth the ride, not for the destination, but for the sweet banana-peel moments you share along the way.

I remember talking with my dad one day about something as simple as the weather. We were deep in the usual chat about rain and sunshine when suddenly, without any warning, he asked, "Remember that time we went to the Grand Canyon?" Now, I'd love to say we had a great family road trip to the Grand Canyon, but here's the funny thing—we never went! Instead of correcting him and slipping on the reality peel, I decided to just go with it. "Oh yeah," I said, "it was beautiful, wasn't it?" And just like that, we were off on a whole adventure, talking about this imaginary vacation we'd never taken. Did it matter that it wasn't real? Not in the slightest. For him, it was as real as the rain outside, and the joy of reminiscing about this non-existent trip was a moment we got to share together.

The message here? Let go of the need to be right—of trying to keep the conversation on track—there's no use in trying to peel the banana too perfectly. With dementia, the conversation doesn't have to have a clear beginning or end, and that's okay. You're there for the ride, not the destination. The real magic happens when you stop worrying about whether the story is factually accurate and start embracing the beauty of where the moment takes you, whether that's a ripe memory or a green one still finding its sweetness.

Embrace the Moment, Not the Logic

In our day-to-day lives, we're used to making sure conversations make sense, that stories have a point, or that we're leading to some kind of conclusion. But with dementia, logic takes a back seat, like slipping on a banana peel and landing somewhere unexpected—and honestly, there's something freeing about that. Conversations become less about sticking to reality and more about enjoying the ride, whether that means hopping from lunch to childhood stories or ending up on a wild trip to an imaginary beach.

One of the gifts dementia brings is the opportunity to live entirely in the moment. Your loved one might not remember where the conversation started, and they certainly won't care if it makes sense. What they care about is the connection they feel in that moment with you. And when you let go of trying to guide the conversation back to the "right" topic, you'll find that the ride is a lot more fun—like slipping on a banana peel and laughing at where you land.

The Fantasy Vacation: Letting Them Lead

Here's a tip: let them lead the way. If your loved one starts talking about something that never happened, don't feel the need to steer

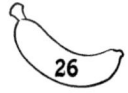

them back to reality—just peel away your expectations and join them in their fantasy. I call this the "Fantasy Vacation" technique, where you just go along for the ride, no matter where it leads.

Imagine you're talking with your mom, and she suddenly starts reminiscing about the time she went to the moon (yes, the moon!). Now, you could try to correct her and say, "Mom, you've never been to space," but where's the fun in that? Instead, lean in and ask, "What was it like up there?" You might be surprised at the joy and creativity that comes from her response. By embracing the fantasy, you're showing her that you value the connection more than the facts, and that's what really matters. Besides, who wouldn't want to hear about space from someone with their own banana-flavored twist?

Memory Loops: It's About the Emotion, Not the Details

One of the hardest things about dementia is watching your loved one forget the details of their life, especially when it comes to shared memories. But here's the thing—while the facts might slip away, the emotions don't. Your dad might not remember what year it was when you took that trip to the beach, but he'll remember the feeling of joy, the sound of the waves, or the warmth of the sun. And that's the part you want to hold onto.

I once had a conversation with my dad where he got halfway through telling me about his favorite movie but couldn't remember the title or the plot. He stopped and said, "Wait, what was I saying?" I could see the frustration slipping onto his face, and instead of trying to help him fill in the blanks, I shifted the focus. "You were talking about how much you loved that movie. What made you feel so good when you watched it?" His face lit up again as he described the way the film made him laugh. The details didn't matter anymore—what mattered was how it made him feel, and I got to share that feeling with him.

Ride the Roller Coaster, Hands in the Air

Think of memory loops like riding a roller coaster: sometimes the ride goes in circles, sometimes it drops off unexpectedly, and sometimes it takes you to places you didn't even know existed. But here's the key—put your hands in the air and enjoy the ride. When your loved

one forgets where the conversation was headed, don't feel the need to redirect them. Instead, ask them another question. Let them take the conversation in a new direction, maybe down another banana-flavored path.

If they forget what they were saying, that's okay. You're not on this ride to reach a final destination. You're on it to enjoy the shared moments of connection, however brief or fleeting they may be. The twists and turns might feel disorienting at first, but the more you embrace the unpredictability, the more you'll see the beauty in each curve. It's not about avoiding slips on the peels; it's about finding joy in the tumble.

Living in the Now

At its core, dementia teaches us to live in the now. Your loved one isn't thinking about the future or the past—they're existing entirely in the present. And that's where you'll find your connection. Instead of trying to bring them back to where the conversation "should" be, meet them where they are. Whether they're talking about something real or imaginary, whether they remember the details or not, they are sharing a moment with you.

When you stop worrying about the destination and focus on being present, you'll find joy in the journey. It might be a roller coaster ride, full of twists, turns, and the occasional banana peel slip, but every loop brings you closer to the heart of what really matters: being there, in that moment, with them. Embrace the ride.

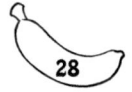

Helpful Tip # 5
Peel Away Expectations. Embrace the Moment.

O ne of the hardest parts of caring for someone with dementia is learning to let go of what you thought things would be like and embracing what is right in front of you. Our expectations—those ideas about how things *should go*—can make dementia care feel frustrating. It's like trying to peel a banana that isn't quite ripe—it's tough, it resists, and the whole process just feels off. But when you start to roll with it when you let go of what you think *should happen*, things begin to flow more easily—even when life gets a little slippery.

The key is to peel away those expectations and live in the moment, just like your loved one does. People with dementia aren't stuck in the past or worried about the future—they're living in the now. And that's where you need to be, too.

The Lego Lesson: Finding Joy in Simplicity

I knew someone whose dad had been a brilliant engineer. He could design complicated machines without breaking a sweat. But when dementia took hold, it gradually stripped away his ability to remember those intricate designs. It broke her heart at first, watching him struggle to remember the very thing that once defined him.

Then, one day, instead of focusing on what he couldn't do, she decided to change things up. She started bringing simple Lego sets during her visits. They built tiny cars and houses together. He may not have been able to design complex engines anymore, but creating something simple brought him joy. It wasn't about trying to get him back to what he used to be—it was about living in the moment, doing something that made him happy. And that was more than enough.

When you peel away your expectations, you can start to appreciate what your loved one *can* do right now. You make room for connection, laughter, and the joy of being in the moment. That's where the magic happens—not in wishing things were different, but in embracing what is.

Rolling With It: How Letting Go of Expectations Frees You

Expectations can build a lot of pressure—pressure to have the perfect visit, the perfect conversation, or that perfect "aha" moment of connection. But when you're dealing with dementia, those expectations can lead to a lot of frustration. Trying to keep things "on track" is like holding onto a peeled banana—slippery, hard to grasp, and ultimately unsatisfying.

Instead of holding on tight to how you think things should go, try loosening your grip. Expecting things to go smoothly or having your loved one act like they used to can set you up for disappointment. But if you go into it expecting the unpredictable—if you're ready for memory lapses, confusion, or silence—you can roll with whatever comes your way. And when you do that, you'll find a lot more grace, love, and peace in the process.

Peeling Back the Layers: Seeing the Joy in the Now

When you peel back those expectations, you uncover joy that's already there. Maybe your loved one gets a bit lost in conversation or repeats the same story again and again. Instead of getting frustrated or trying to pull them back to reality, let go of your need for things to make sense and just be present.

I remember visiting my dad once, and he kept telling me the same story—over and over again, with the same excitement every single time. Instead of reminding him he'd already told me, I just went with it. I asked new questions and let him feel the joy of retelling it, and in that moment, we connected. It wasn't about the content of the story; it was about sharing a moment together.

Embrace the Banana Split Moments

Caregiving can be a lot like making a banana split—messy, unpredictable, and full of surprises. But when you peel away your expectations, you start to see the beauty in that mess. Maybe the conversation didn't flow perfectly, or the activity you planned didn't go quite as expected. That's okay. Those "banana split" moments—when things are a bit scattered but still sweet—are where you'll find the real magic.

Even when things don't go as planned, there's sweetness to be found. Whether it's a messy craft project, a confused conversation, or a shared laugh, these moments are full of love and flavor, and they're worth savoring.

Releasing Control: The Real Gift of Grace

Here's the thing about bananas—and life in general—you can't always control when they're ripe. Trying to control every moment when you're caring for someone with dementia is kind of like trying to stop a banana from turning brown. It's going to happen, and that's okay. At the heart of letting go of expectations is releasing control. You can't control dementia, and you can't control every moment of your loved one's day. But when you let go of that need to control every detail, you find a new kind of freedom—the freedom to simply *be* with your loved one, to love them as they are, and to find beauty in the unexpected.

Peeling away expectations isn't about giving up hope. It's about realizing that the present moment—however imperfect—is where real connection happens. It's about finding joy in the now without holding onto the past or worrying about the future.

The real gift comes when you stop trying to control everything and go with the flow. Letting go of that need for perfection frees you to have fun and enjoy the weird, unexpected, and beautiful moments with your loved one. You don't need everything to be perfect for it to be wonderful.

Grace for You and Them

Letting go of expectations gives you grace, too. It frees you from frustration when things don't go as planned and lets you roll with the situation, laugh at the chaos, and breathe through the tough moments.

So, peel away those expectations. Let go of what you think should happen and instead embrace what *is* happening. Whether it's building Legos, listening to the same story on repeat, or sitting quietly together, these are the moments that matter. These are the moments that will fill your heart long after the banana peels are gone.

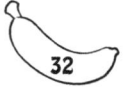

Helpful Tip # 6
Woo-Hoo Moments

Who doesn't love a party? Imagine this: you walk into the room with a plate of freshly baked cookies, and suddenly the whole day lights up. For your loved one with dementia, every little treat is like a woo-hoo moment—a mini celebration. That's the magic of small joys: they turn an ordinary day into a surprise party, one bite at a time. Sprinkle your caregiving journey with woo-hoo confetti, and watch the joy spread.

The Cookie Crumble Theory

Now, let's dive into The Cookie Crumble Theory. Picture this: you're biting into a cookie, and the crumbs go everywhere. At first, it seems a bit messy, right? But here's the thing—those crumbs are still part of the cookie, part of the joy. In caregiving, it's the same. The tiny, simple pleasures—whether it's a cookie, a cozy blanket, or a song that makes them tap their feet—might seem like small moments, but each little "crumb" of joy adds up to something much bigger.

Even if that joy only lasts for a few minutes, it's a win. The cookie might crumble, but those small pieces still pack a lot of sweetness. Each smile, each moment of calm or laughter, is like gathering up those cookie crumbs and savoring every bit. You don't need a perfect whole cookie to celebrate. Those crumbs—those tiny moments of joy—are worth celebrating every single time. It's like pulling the string on a party popper, where the confetti only lasts for a few seconds, but it brightens the whole room.

So, embrace the crumbs. Let each tiny moment of joy remind you that even in the midst of caregiving chaos, there's always room for sweetness, celebration, and love—one cookie crumb at a time.

Cookies, Sweaters, and Tunes—Oh My!

My dad loved chocolate chip cookies—the soft, chewy, gooey kind. Just like bananas, every time I brought him freshly baked cookies, he would exclaim, "These are the best cookies I've ever had!" even if he had said the same thing five minutes earlier. But here's the secret: it wasn't about the cookie; it was about experiencing the joy of it, again and again. Every bite was a brand-new treat, every time. These moments are like little balloons of joy you get to keep tossing into the air. The more you sprinkle them throughout the day, the more you turn everyday moments into a confetti-covered celebration.

It's not just about the treat itself—it's about creating an atmosphere of celebration, even in the smallest ways. Whether it's a warm cup of tea, the smell of lavender, or a familiar tune playing on repeat, these small treats aren't just extras—they're the main event. The real party is in the moments when you see their eyes light up. These little celebrations aren't just small wins—they're the heartbeat of your caregiving journey.

The Cookie Party Theory: Keep the Treats Coming!

Here's where it gets fun: the treats never have to stop! Every visit, every conversation, you get to offer a new little treat—like a never-ending party where the confetti keeps falling. Maybe it's cookies today,

a box of chocolates tomorrow, or a cozy chat about the weather. The point is, it's not about the grand gestures; it's about those tiny moments that make them feel special.

Think of your loved one's day like a series of surprise party favors. Each treat, each shared laugh, is a little package of joy you get to open together. If your loved one loves cookies, bring the cookies. If they get excited about their favorite song, play it on repeat. Even if it feels like you're throwing the same party over and over, they're having the time of their life every single time.

Turning Small Wins into Big Wins

The magic of these small moments is that they create a ripple effect of happiness. It's like that first cookie crumble—it leads to another, and before you know it, you've turned an ordinary moment into something sweet and memorable. These small wins add up, creating a mosaic of joyful moments that brighten their day and lift your spirits, too.

When you embrace The Cookie Crumble Theory, you're giving your loved one the gift of repeated joy. You're turning what could be an ordinary moment into something worth celebrating. Every cookie, every cuddle, and every laugh are reminders that life, even with dementia, is full of surprises, wins, and love.

The Party Never Ends: Keep Throwing Confetti

The beauty of dementia care is that every moment is new and fresh. Sure, the road can get tough, and there are days when things feel overwhelming, but when you start looking for those *woo-hoo* moments, you'll realize how much joy can be found in the little things. Keep throwing confetti, keep passing out the cookies, and keep celebrating the wins—big and small.

So, what's your next treat? Whatever it is, serve it up with love and watch the magic happen. With the *Cookie Crumble theory*, joy is endless, wins are real, and the party never stops! Woo-hoo! And don't forget the ice cream!

Helpful Tip # 7
Repainting the Past

Dementia has this incredible way of **reshuffling memories,** blending pieces of the past in ways that might seem confusing to us but make perfect sense to them. Your loved one might recall events that never happened or mix up details from their life. Instead of worrying about making the painting "right," this chapter is about letting them repaint their history and live in their version of reality—with grace, love, and creativity.

Imagine walking into a room where your loved one is painting a new picture of their past. Maybe it's filled with wild stories or details that don't quite match up. But does it really matter? What matters is the connection and shared experience. Your role isn't to correct them—it's to embrace their story and let them live in it fully.

Home Runs with Mickey Mantle

Take my dad, for example. One day, he confidently told me about the time he played baseball with Mickey Mantle. Did I point out that he'd never been to a baseball game, let alone met one of the greatest players? Nope! I jumped right in with him: "Wow, Dad, you hit a home run off Mickey Mantle? That's incredible!" We spent the next half-hour talking about his "legendary" sports career, laughing and bonding over a story that wasn't technically real—but felt real in that moment.

The lesson? It's not about being right. It's about allowing them to live in their world and celebrating the joy that comes from that. By letting them repaint the past in their own way, you're giving them the freedom to feel empowered and proud in their story.

Let Them Hold the Brush

We all like to think of our memories as unchangeable records of our lives, but dementia changes that. Instead of getting frustrated when they mix up dates or places, let them hold the brush and create their version of the past. If they insist they traveled to Paris in the 1950s (even though they never left their hometown), don't correct them. Ask them about the Eiffel Tower or how the croissants tasted. Their version of reality is no less valid just because it's different from yours. In fact, it's the only reality that matters at that moment.

The Art of Going Along for the Ride

It can be tempting to correct your loved one, especially when their stories are way off. But correction often leads to frustration. Instead of trying to bring them back to your version of the past, step into theirs. One woman told me about her mother, who "remembered" being a famous Hollywood actress. Rather than correcting her, she asked questions like, "What was your favorite movie to star in?" Her mother's joy in talking about her glamorous life was priceless. By going along for the ride, she gave her mom the chance to feel like a star—even if only for a while.

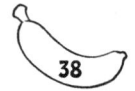

Giving Yourself Grace

Caregiving can be exhausting, especially when their stories change from one visit to the next. It's natural to want to ground the conversation in reality, but sometimes, the best way to help is by letting go of the need to be right. Give yourself the grace to let the stories flow without correction. Every time they repaint the past, it's a chance for connection, a moment to see the world through their eyes.

The Freedom of a New Story

For your loved one, living in a world where memories constantly shift can be unsettling. By allowing them to repaint the past, you're giving them freedom—the freedom to create, to imagine, and to feel in control of their story, even as it changes. Sometimes, that creativity will surprise you with wild "adventures" they've never had. But instead of focusing on the fact that these stories aren't true, embrace the excitement and connection they bring.

The Real Connection: Living in the Moment

At the heart of this chapter is the idea of grace—for them and you. The connection you build doesn't depend on getting the details right. Whether they're telling you about playing baseball with Mickey Mantle or starring in a Hollywood film, what matters is being present with them in that moment.

The masterpiece isn't in the accuracy—it's in the connection you create while sharing in their world. So, the next time your loved one starts to repaint the past, don't reach for the correction brush. Instead, help them paint the scene and enjoy the journey together.

A CAREGIVER'S ODE TO BANANAS

In the land of caregiving, where love never sleeps,
There's a secret ingredient that everyone keeps.
It's not found in textbooks or courses or scans,
It's the wisdom of bananas right there in your hands!

When days get tough, and your patience runs thin,
Just think of the peel and where you've been.
You've handled it all, from the sweet to the bruised,
And with each slip-up, you've still been amused.

Gratitude grows like bananas on trees,
A simple "thank you" floats on the breeze.
From flowers to notes, even a smile can do,
The care team feels seen, and they care back for you!

And when it gets hard, as it sometimes will,
You handle the hiccups with humor and skill.
If the day feels rotten, like a bruised old peel,
Just mash it into bread—that's a sweet deal!

The caregivers work with quiet might,
Through holiday cheer and long, tough nights.
A small act of kindness can make their day,
Like offering bananas on a bright silver tray!

But let's not forget, on this wild, wacky ride,
It's not all about work—there's fun on the side!
From Halloween treats to pranks full of flair,
Bananas remind us to laugh and care.

So, here's to the caregivers, the givers, the crew,
The bananas of wisdom we share with you.

40

Through ups and downs, we peel back the layers,
With love, laughter, and banana prayers!

Banana wisdom, tried and true,
Because life's just sweeter with a banana or two!

~*David Lloyd Strauss*

Helpful Tip # 8
How Music Keeps the Memories Alive

You know that feeling when your favorite upbeat song comes on, and suddenly, you can't help but feel the energy rushing through your body? Maybe you start tapping your feet, drumming your knees, and before you know it, you're totally lost in the rhythm. Well, people with dementia experience that same connection to music, too, but for them, it can be even more profound. It's like a lifeline to memories that feel just out of reach, sparking moments of recognition in ways words sometimes can't.

There's something truly magical about music. It has the power to touch places in the heart and mind that words fail to reach, especially for those living with dementia. Even when names, faces, and details fade, a familiar melody can cut through the fog, transporting your loved one to a cherished moment from the past.

Music doesn't just stir up memories; it unlocks emotions buried deep, creating a bridge to moments that might otherwise seem lost. Music is a secret antidote to mental and emotional connection. It's all about tapping into that magic—using music to bring joy, spark memories, and connect with your loved one, even when other forms of communication become difficult.

For my dad, music was like an anchor. He was an auctioneer, and naturally, he loved "The Auctioneer" by Leroy Van Dyke—a song that perfectly reflected his passion and energy. Every time he heard it, his face would light up, and he'd tap along to the beat as if he were back at the auction stand, commanding the room. Another favorite was "How Are Things in Glocca Morra" by Buddy Clark. This song would take him somewhere special, like visiting an old, familiar place in his heart. Even when he struggled to remember the day-to-day details, the music was always there, grounding him and bringing him peace and happiness.

But my dad's real instrument of choice was his voice—and not just for singing, but for *yodeling*. He was a master yodeler. Even though he couldn't always sing on tune, he could yodel like nobody else. I still remember him yodeling while walking with my sister and me through Central Park. It wasn't just something he did as a quirky habit—he yodeled his entire life. That's how deeply music, and yodeling in particular, was woven into who he was. His ability to yodel, combined with his endless library of limericks, filled our lives with laughter and joy. Even when dementia began to change his world, the yodeling never stopped. It was like his way of holding onto himself, his way of saying, "I'm still here."

The Magic of a Personalized Playlist

Music therapy is one of the most powerful tools for caregivers. Creating a personalized playlist for your loved one can be like giving them a key to their most cherished memories. Think of it as the *playlist of their life*, filled with songs that have meaning—tunes that remind them of their childhood, favorite holidays, or even their career, like my dad's connection to "The Auctioneer." Each song is like a time capsule, waiting to bring a forgotten smile or spark an old memory.

For my dad, that playlist would always include "The Auctioneer," "How Are Things in Glocca Morra," and some good yodeling songs to boot! Even when other forms of connection faded, music would still reach him. And, of course, I had to throw in a few of his favorite limericks for good measure—because if there was ever a chance to get him laughing, it was through a well-timed limerick.

Crafting the Ultimate Playlist

So, how do you create the perfect playlist for your loved one? It's all about knowing their story and finding the songs that were the soundtrack to their life. Here are a few tips to get started:

1. **Go Back in Time:** Start with the music from their youth. What songs were popular when they were growing up? Did they have a favorite band or artist? For my dad, Buddy Clark was one of those voices that could instantly take him back to a simpler time. Ask them (if they can remember) about the music they loved when they were younger, or chat with other family members who might know.

2. **Connect to Their Hobbies or Career:** In my dad's case, "The Auctioneer" wasn't just a fun tune—it was a reminder of his life's work. If your loved one had a particular passion or career that can be tied to a song, include it. Whether it's a song they used to dance to, a piece of classical music they loved, or even something tied to their profession, these songs can become emotional triggers that unlock old memories.

3. **Holiday Hits and Family Favorites:** Holiday music and songs that were played during family gatherings can also have a strong impact. In the same way Christmas carols might bring you back to decorating the tree as a kid, these songs can transport your loved one to a place of warmth and joy, even when other memories are hard to grasp.

4. **Sing-Along Songs:** Include songs that are easy to sing along with—or, in my dad's case, songs he could yodel along with! Whether it's a catchy tune or an old favorite, the act of singing (or yodeling) together creates connection and fun, even if they don't get every word right.

When Words Fail, Music and Yodeling Speak

One of the most remarkable things about music—and yodeling—is how it bypasses the need for words. Even when your loved one struggles to communicate, music has a way of speaking directly to their heart. You don't need to remind them of who they used to be or where they are now—just let the music do the talking. Let the playlist serve as a bridge between the past and the present, reminding them of the joy, love, and happiness they've experienced throughout their life.

Even when my dad didn't always know who was sitting next to him, I could see that spark of recognition in his eyes when one of his favorite songs or a good yodeling tune came on. It was like flipping through an old photo album, but instead of pictures, it was melodies that brought those memories back into focus.

A Soundtrack of Grace

Music is a gift, not only for your loved one but also for you. It allows you to create moments of connection, even when words fail. It gives your loved one the grace to live in the world as they remember it—where they're still yodeling through Central Park, reciting limericks, singing their favorite songs, and smiling at the sound of a familiar melody.

By creating a playlist, you're giving them more than just music—you're giving them access to a part of their soul that dementia can't take away. So, turn up the music, let it play, and let the songs remind them—and you—of the life they've lived and the joy that's still very much alive within them.

Woo-hoo! It's time to dance, yodel, and sing along!

Helpful Tip # 9
Just Being There—Matters

S ometimes, the most valuable thing you can offer your loved one with dementia isn't a conversation, an activity, or even a carefully crafted playlist—it's simply your presence. The art of doing nothing can be more profound than any words or actions. This chapter is about letting go of the pressure to fill every moment and embracing the idea that just *being* with your loved one is more than enough. The quiet moments of stillness, sitting in silence, or holding their hand speak volumes, even when words don't.

I remember one particular visit with my dad. He didn't feel like talking much that day. Instead of trying to fill the silence with conversation or an activity, we sat together, quietly watching the birds outside his window. At first, it felt strange not to talk, but soon, I realized that my presence was what mattered. He was at ease, simply knowing I was there. We didn't need to share stories or laughter at that moment—just sitting there and watching the world outside brought a sense of peace.

It was a powerful reminder that sometimes, doing nothing is the most meaningful act of all.

It's easy to feel like you need to be "doing" something to make your time together meaningful. You might feel pressure to keep the conversation going, to create an activity, or to make sure your visit is "productive." But here's the truth: *presence* is the most powerful gift you can give. Simply being there, even in the quiet, has a way of grounding your loved one. It lets them know they are not alone, even if they can't express it in words.

Sometimes, words aren't necessary for connection. In fact, as dementia progresses, words may become harder for your loved one to find. But that doesn't mean the connection is lost. Sitting quietly together can be just as meaningful as a deep conversation. There's comfort in the simplicity of silent companionship. The warmth of your hand, the sound of your breathing, the shared view of birds outside the window—these small things create a deep bond that words sometimes can't touch.

In those quiet moments, stillness can act like music, too, offering a kind of background melody that brings peace. It's like the moments between the notes of a song—the pauses are just as important as the music itself. In these pauses, your loved one can feel the calm, the grace, and the love that exists without needing to be spoken.

Sometimes, my dad and I didn't need a yodel or a limerick to fill the space. It was enough to sit quietly and listen to the sounds around us. The birds became our soundtrack, the breeze through the window our melody. There was no pressure to create anything beyond the present moment, and in that stillness, we found a connection.

It's easy to feel like silence is awkward or unproductive, but the truth is, there's grace in those quiet moments. It's in the stillness that we find a deeper sense of presence, both for ourselves and for our loved ones. When you let go of the need to fill the silence, you create space for something more profound: a sense of peace, a shared experience, and a connection that goes beyond words.

The Real Art of Doing Nothing

The art of doing nothing isn't about *literally* doing nothing—it's about creating a space of calm, love, and connection in the simplest of ways. Whether it's holding hands, sitting in silence, or just being a comforting presence, these moments are as valuable—if not more so—than any activity you could plan. It's about *being* instead of *doing*, and in that being, you give your loved one the greatest gift of all: peace.

So, next time you feel the need to "do" something, remember that just *being* there matters. Whether you're sitting in silence, watching birds, or simply holding their hand, your presence is enough. You are enough. And in that quiet, still space, there's more connection than words could ever express.

Helpful Tip # 10
The Magic of Old Photos

Old photos can be more than just pieces of paper—they're windows into the past, little portals that can unlock memories, even when words and details seem lost. For someone living with dementia, those familiar faces, places, and moments captured in photographs can spark something inside, bringing a sense of comfort, joy, and connection. This chapter is all about how using old photos can stimulate conversation, bring laughter, and, most importantly, help your loved one feel alive and connected to their story.

One of my favorite experiences with my dad involved an old family album that my sister put together for him. He didn't remember every name or event in the pictures, but he lit up at the sight of familiar smiles and laughter. We spent the afternoon flipping through the album, chuckling over old hairstyles, vintage outfits, and long-forgotten moments. What stood out wasn't that he could recall every detail but that he recognized the *feeling* in those pictures—the joy on people's faces, the warmth of family gatherings, the sense of belonging. Even when the stories he told didn't line up with reality, the photos helped bring him to life.

Photos have a way of bypassing some of the barriers dementia creates, tapping into emotional memories rather than factual ones. Even if your loved one doesn't recall the names of everyone in the photo or the exact event it captured, they will likely remember how they felt at that moment. And that's where the magic lies—helping them connect to the *emotion* of the memory.

You might show your loved one a photo of them at a family reunion and notice how they smile or soften at the sight of familiar faces. Maybe they don't remember exactly who was there, but they remember that it was a happy occasion. Or, like my dad, they may laugh at their own goofy expressions or remember a specific detail like "That was the best barbecue ever!" even if the rest of the memory is unclear.

Photos from their younger years or family snapshots with their children, grandchildren, or even pets are always a big hit. When you find a photo that makes them smile or laugh, draw attention to it. Let them linger on it. Encourage them to talk about what they remember or how the photo makes them feel.

Sometimes, the stories they tell won't match the reality, and that's okay. It's not about being right—it's about letting them create a connection to the past, even if the details are blurry. The act of storytelling, of sharing their version of events, helps them feel alive and engaged in their own story.

For my dad, one of his favorite pictures was of him on his bicycle. He loved cycling as much as a flower loves sunshine. Every time he saw a picture of himself on his bicycle, he'd tell stories about how he flew to Italy to have his bike custom-built, which is a true story.

Photos have a way of bringing back not just memories but laughter, too. I remember flipping through a family album with my dad and coming across an old picture of him with a mustache that could only be described as... *unique*. We both burst out laughing, and for the next few minutes, the conversation turned into a playful roast of old fashion choices. Even though the memory of when the picture was taken was hazy, the laughter was real, the connection genuine.

Old photos have the power to bring humor into a situation that can sometimes feel heavy. Looking at pictures of family vacations, holiday dinners, or birthday parties can lead to laughter over mishaps, outfits that didn't age well, or silly moments that were captured forever. And when you and your loved one are laughing together, those are the moments when you're both fully present, connected not by the past but by the magic of now.

Photos are also a great tool for encouraging storytelling. When your loved one sees an old picture, give them the floor. Let them tell you what they remember, even if the story changes each time.

When they share their memories, no matter how altered they may be, they're reclaiming a piece of themselves. The act of recalling, of sharing, gives them a sense of autonomy, of being in control of their life. That feeling is priceless. You don't have to correct them or steer them back to the "true" version of events—just let them enjoy the ride of their own memory, no matter where it takes them.

For my dad, it didn't matter that the details were fuzzy. What mattered was the pride he felt when he told the story of his auctioneering days or the warmth in his voice when he reminisced about old family gatherings. The photos acted as a springboard for him to dive into his own recollections, and that brought him a sense of joy and purpose.

There's something special about the way old photos help us relive cherished memories, but they also allow us to create new moments. When you sit with your loved one, flipping through albums and talking about the past, you're not just revisiting memories—you're creating new ones. Even if they don't remember the conversation tomorrow, in that moment, they feel alive, connected, and seen.

Capturing Their Spirit

Old photos capture not just moments but the essence of who your loved one was and still is. Even as dementia takes away certain memories or abilities, those photos remind you (and them) of the vibrant, full life they've lived. Whether it's a snapshot of them laughing at a family picnic, holding you as a baby, or proudly standing in front of their first home, these images are a testament to their spirit, their love, and their legacy.

When you bring those photos into the present, you're helping them reconnect with the best parts of their past. You're saying, "I see you. I remember you. You're still here." And for someone living with dementia, that feeling of being seen and remembered is more powerful than any words could convey.

So, the next time you visit your loved one, bring along an old photo album. Flip through the pages, let them point out their favorite pictures, and listen as they tell their stories. The photos may be old, but the connection they create is very much alive.

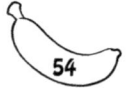

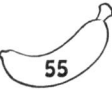

Helpful Tip # 11
Games That Are More Than Just Fun

You know that feeling when you're playing a game with a friend, and suddenly it becomes less about the game and more about the laughs? That's what it's like when you're playing games with someone who has dementia—it's all about the connection, not the rules. Games aren't just for kids; they're little windows of happiness that can bring smiles, laughter, and even a sense of accomplishment to your loved one.

I mean, let's face it: caregiving can feel heavy, so why not lighten things up with a simple deck of cards, a puzzle, or even a coloring book? I used to play a matching game with my dad, and each time he made a match, we'd throw a mini celebration like he'd just won the lottery. High-fives, clapping, laughter—it wasn't about "winning" the game. It was about creating a moment where he could feel *good*. And those little victories? They're pure gold.

Let Them Win—and Make it Count. Now, I know what you might be thinking: "But isn't letting them win kind of cheating?" Not at all! Letting your loved one win isn't about rigging the game; it's about giving them a well-deserved boost. When they make that match or finish a puzzle, you're not just celebrating the win—you're celebrating *them*. It's a way for them to feel successful in a world that might seem confusing or uncertain. So, the next time your loved one pulls off a victory—even a small one—cheer like you're at a championship game. Trust me, that sense of pride and happiness is totally worth it.

One of the best parts of playing games with my dad was seeing how his face would light up with every win. We'd laugh and clap together like he'd just aced the hardest test in the world. And the pride? Oh, you could see it in his eyes. These small wins weren't just about playing a game—they were about him feeling like he still had it. And honestly, that's what it's all about.

Not everyone's going to be into matching games, and that's totally fine. Maybe your loved one enjoys a simple game of Go Fish, or maybe it's puzzles, coloring, or even stacking blocks. The key is finding something that makes them smile and feel successful without stressing over the rules.

I once knew a woman whose mom loved cards. Even when she couldn't remember all the rules, they still had a blast. The rules were just "suggestions" by that point, but the fun? That was real. And every time her mom *won*, the celebration was epic. Because, really, it wasn't about the cards at all—it was her feeling like a winner.

Celebrate Like Every Win is a Big Deal

Here's the secret sauce: the celebration! It's not enough just to let them win—you've got to make a *big deal* out of it. Clap, cheer, high-five, do a little dance if you want! The point is to make them feel like a champion, because those moments of excitement and joy are what make the game so special. You're not just playing; you're creating a memory that both of you will hold onto.

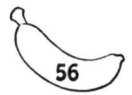

Keep the Hands Busy, and the Heart Happy

Sometimes, it's not even about winning. For some loved ones, the best "games" are the ones that keep their hands busy—coloring, knitting, crafting, or even just stacking blocks. It's not about completing a task; it's about giving them something fun to do that keeps them engaged and happy.

I knew someone whose mom loved to knit but couldn't manage it anymore. So, they swapped knitting for coloring, and you know what? It worked! Filling in bright patterns became a source of pride, and those small creative moments brought joy without any competition involved.

Bend the Rules, Make it Fun

Not all games need to follow the strict rulebook. Sometimes, you've got to bend the rules a little (or a lot) to make it fun for your loved one. Maybe you use fewer cards, leave the pairs face up, or let them take extra turns. Whatever keeps it enjoyable and stress-free.

I used to tweak our matching game to make it easier for my dad. We'd use fewer cards, leave them face up, and focus on having fun. Every match he made was another victory, another high five, and another chance to make him feel like he was the king of the game.

Games are more than just something to pass the time. They're a way to celebrate and create happy moments that mean so much in the caregiving journey. When you let them win and cheer them on, you're not just playing—you're giving them a gift. It's the gift of feeling accomplished, loved, and happy. And those are the moments that stick with you both.

So, next time you sit down for a game, let your loved one win. Make it fun, laugh a little louder, and cheer a little harder. Because when it comes down to it, every small win is a big victory in the world of dementia care. Woo-hoo! Here's to more high-fives, more laughter, and a whole lot of joy.

Helpful Tip # 12
The Long Goodbye Finding Peace in the Slow Moments

Dementia is known as a long, slow goodbye. It's a journey for both of you and not always easy. But that doesn't mean the path is without beauty. In fact, some of the most meaningful moments come in the quiet, unspoken spaces.

I remember one day vividly. My dad didn't recognize me at all. His eyes searched my face, but the recognition wasn't there. Still, when I handed him a banana—his favorite—he smiled. It was such a simple, fleeting thing, but that smile meant the world to me. It wasn't about whether he knew my name or understood the moment; it was about the connection we shared in that small gesture. That smile was a reminder that love is still there, even when memories aren't.

The Journey Is Theirs—But You Walk Beside Them

Your loved one is on their own journey, and it's a path that may not look like the one you're walking. They are winding down the chapters of their life story, but that doesn't mean they're lost. You are there to help them finish that story with dignity, with love, and with as much peace and happiness as possible. It's about being present, not to fix or change what's happening, but to walk beside them as they move through this final chapter.

Imagine, for a moment, how you'd want someone to be there for you when your own life story begins to wind down. You wouldn't want them to be frustrated because you've forgotten names or lost track of time. You'd want them to be patient and to help you feel seen and loved no matter what.

Finding Beauty in the Slow Moments

Dementia slows everything down. Conversations don't flow like they used to; memories come and go, and the pace of life changes. But this slower rhythm isn't something to resist—it's something to embrace. In the stillness, in the quiet, in the pauses between words and memories, there's room to find a different kind of connection.

One day, I sat with my dad in silence. He wasn't in the mood for conversation, and that was okay. We didn't need to fill the time with words. Instead, we just sat together, watching the birds outside his window. And though there were no deep conversations or shared stories that day, the peace I felt being there with him was profound. It was a reminder that being *with* someone is more powerful than anything you can say or do. Simply *being there* is an act of love, and it's a way of showing your loved one that they are not alone on this journey.

Giving Them Grace, and Giving Yourself Grace

This journey isn't just about finding peace for your loved one—it's also about finding peace for yourself. Caring for someone with dementia can be emotionally exhausting, but the key is to give yourself grace. It's okay to feel sadness, frustration, and grief as you walk this road. But remember, you are doing something beautiful. You are helping your

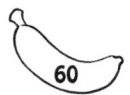

loved one write the last pages of their life story, and that is a sacred task.

As the moments slow down and your loved one drifts further from the world they once knew, give yourself permission to let go of what "should" be and embrace what *is*. It's okay if some days are harder than others. It's okay if all you have to give is your presence. That is enough.

Just as you would want someone to help you wind down your own life story, offer that same grace to your loved one. Be there in the slow moments, and trust that those small acts of love are writing a beautiful, dignified ending to their story.

Dementia may feel like a long, slow goodbye, but it's also a journey of love. Every moment, every smile, every small gesture is part of that goodbye. Even if your loved one doesn't remember who you are, they can still feel your love. They still know, on some deep level, that you are there, walking beside them.

This long goodbye isn't about loss—it's about finding peace in the winding down of life's story. It's about learning to appreciate the beauty of each moment, no matter how small. And just as you'd hope for someone to do for you one day, you are giving your loved one the greatest gift of all: the gift of dignity, of love, and of being fully present as they complete their journey.

So, as you sit with them, hand them their favorite treat, share a quiet moment, or simply be present, know that you're doing something extraordinary. You are part of their story, helping them wind it down with grace. And when the journey feels slow or difficult, remember it's in these slow moments that the deepest connections are made. This is the long goodbye, but it's also a long journey of love.

Helpful Tip # 13
Holiday Fun—Making Memories That Shine

Holidays are magical times for everyone, and that magic doesn't fade just because your loved one is in a memory care facility. In fact, the holidays are the perfect opportunity to bring that magic directly to them, and the joy that follows can light up their world. The truth is, they might not know it's Halloween, Chanukah, Christmas, or New Year's unless you show them. But the beauty is in seeing how these little reminders can spark joy and help reconnect them to deeply buried memories of holiday fun and happiness.

Bring the Fun to Them

When you arrive to visit your loved one, don't just bring yourself—bring the holidays with you! Assisted living and memory care facilities go all out with decorations and parties for the holidays, but you can

add your personal touch. A little tinsel, a few paper snowflakes, or some pumpkins and fall leaves can go a long way. Even if your loved one doesn't fully understand what's going on, the festive environment will help them feel the warmth and excitement.

One of the best things you can do is simply participate. Join in on the holiday parties that the facility hosts. When you show up for these events, it means the world to both your loved one and the caregivers. I always made it a point to be there for my dad's holiday parties. My sister and I would bring gifts, deck out his room with decorations, and help make the space feel as festive as possible. The memories of watching him—and all the residents—celebrating, laughing, and soaking in the holiday cheer are some of my fondest memories. It's not about making everything perfect; it's about making the moment feel special.

You don't have to go overboard to make a holiday visit special. It's the small, thoughtful gestures that mean the most. Bring a few Santa hats and stand in front of a mirror with them, laughing at how festive you both look. Snap a few pictures—those goofy grins in holiday gear will become some of your favorite keepsakes. You could also bring a bag of their favorite holiday treats, something that connects them to their past. For my dad, it was all about chocolate-covered bananas at Christmas, and just seeing the box in his hands would light up his face.

On Halloween, make it silly. Bring some fun costumes, even if it's just a simple mask or a funny hat. Watching your loved one laugh at the sight of a ridiculous pair of bunny ears or a witch's hat will lift your spirits, too. They might not know it's Halloween, but the laughter and joy—it's universal and priceless. And don't forget to bring some holiday music along. Grab your smartphone, queue up a playlist, and fill the room with festive songs. You'll be amazed at how quickly music can change the atmosphere and get everyone into the holiday spirit.

Create the Atmosphere

A lot of memories are tied to our senses, and there's nothing quite like the smell or taste of a favorite holiday treat to bring back a flood of good feelings. Think about what your loved one used to enjoy during the holidays—whether it's gingerbread cookies, potato latkes, eggnog, or peppermint candies—and bring it with you on your next visit. Even

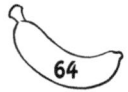

if they don't fully remember the holiday, the taste of those familiar treats might bring a smile to their face and stir up feelings of warmth and comfort.

And don't forget the power of holiday music. Playing a few familiar tunes can instantly brighten their day. Maybe your mom used to sing Christmas carols with you, or your dad loved the sound of Maoz Tzur during Chanukah. Play those songs, sing along, and encourage them to join in. Even if they don't remember all the words, the familiar melody might bring a sense of peace and connection.

In addition to music, think about your loved one's favorite holiday shows or movies. Was your dad a fan of *It's a Wonderful Life* or *A Christmas Story*? Did your mom always laugh along with *A Charlie Brown Christmas* or *Rudolph the Red-Nosed Reindeer*? Or maybe they cherished lighting the menorah while listening to traditional Chanukah songs. Sitting down to watch one of these holiday classics can transport them back to a time when these films and traditions were part of their yearly celebrations. It's not just about the movie or ritual itself—it's about the warmth that comes with reliving a shared holiday experience.

Make the Holidays Their Own

Remember, the holidays are all about connection. If your loved one enjoys a particular tradition, bring it to them. Maybe they loved decorating the tree—bring a small tabletop tree and let them hang a few ornaments. Maybe they always baked cookies for Christmas— bring a batch with you and let them enjoy the familiar smell and taste. The idea is to make the holiday feel like their own, even if it's in a smaller, more manageable way.

For Halloween, consider bringing a few fun-sized candy bars to share, or if they enjoyed handing out candy, get some to pass around to other residents. For New Year's, show up with party hats and noisemakers, even if you're just celebrating quietly together. The key is to create moments of joy that feel true to the way they used to celebrate.

Don't forget to capture those special moments. Snap photos of your loved one in their holiday hat or record a quick video of them laughing at the funny costumes or singing along to their favorite holiday tune.

These are the moments that you'll hold onto later, the memories that will bring a smile to your face long after the holidays are over.

For me, some of my favorite videos are the ones I took during holiday parties with my dad. Watching him laugh, seeing him surrounded by decorations, and knowing he was in a happy place—those memories are priceless. And when I look back on them now, it's as if those moments are still alive, allowing me to enjoy the memory without the responsibilities of caregiving. So, take those pictures and record those videos. You'll be grateful you did.

Celebrate with All Your Heart. Holidays in memory care might look different than they did in the past, but that doesn't mean they can't be filled with joy and connection. At the end of the day, it's about making the holidays as fun and meaningful as you can. Your loved one may not know the holiday is happening without you, but when you show up with that festive spirit, you're giving them the chance to feel the joy of the season once again.

So, put on the Santa hat, cue up the Christmas tunes, light those candles, and celebrate with all your heart. Because these are the moments you'll treasure forever, and these are the memories that will stay with you long after the decorations come down.

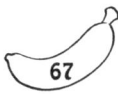

Helpful Tip # 14
Turning Frustration into Fun

Caring for someone with dementia isn't always filled with smiles and banana conversations. There are times when frustration creeps in—sometimes from you, sometimes from them. And let's face it, those moments can be tough. Whether it's confusion that leads to anger or just a bad day, tempers can flare, and feelings can get hurt. But here's where a little creativity, patience, and a good sense of humor can make all the difference.

I learned with my dad that when he got frustrated or upset, it was almost never about what was actually happening at the moment. I was the confusion that came with forgetting something or feeling lost in a familiar place. In those moments, the best thing I could do was help him redirect that energy somewhere else—preferably somewhere fun or at least more peaceful. I would bring up a favorite memory, ask him to sing a song, or, of course, ask him if he wanted a banana.

The Gentle Redirect is all it takes. Think of the gentle redirect as a bit of a game. When your loved one is stuck in a frustrating loop, your job is to help them change the channel—without them even realizing it. You're like the world's best magician, pulling their attention away from the frustration and giving them something lighter to focus on.

The trick is to make the transition smooth. If they're upset because they can't find something, don't argue about whether it's lost—offer to help look for it, even if you know it's already tucked away. Along the way, casually introduce a new topic: "Hey, while we're at it, have you seen this photo of you at the beach? Look how happy you are!" Suddenly, the missing object doesn't seem quite as important anymore.

My sister put together a brilliant photo album from different stages of our dad's life, which he always kept on the side of his bed. It was perfect for redirecting. "Remember that time...," and I'd show him a photo. Voila! Back in his happy place.

One of the best tools for redirecting frustration is humor. When things get tense, don't be afraid to get a little silly. I found that sometimes, the quickest way to pull someone out of a bad mood is by making them laugh. You don't have to be a stand-up comedian—just lighthearted enough to break the tension.

One day, my dad was getting really agitated because he couldn't remember where he put his reading glasses (they were on his head, of course). I knew telling him that outright would just frustrate him more, so instead, I grabbed a pair of sunglasses from my bag and put them on. "Hey, Dad," I said, "maybe I'm the one who stole your glasses!" He stopped, looked at me, and burst out laughing. At that moment, the frustration melted away, and suddenly, we were in on the joke together. It wasn't about the glasses anymore—it was about the moment we shared.

Sometimes, all it takes to redirect frustration is a little distraction. If your loved one is getting worked up over something that's out of your control, it's okay to gently steer the conversation somewhere else. Ask them about a favorite memory, put on some music they love, or offer them a snack. It might sound too simple, but little distractions can be lifesavers when emotions run high.

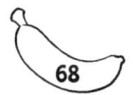

If your loved one is upset because they think they need to be somewhere (even though they don't), try this: instead of arguing or correcting them, say something like, "Let's grab a snack before we go." Nine times out of ten, the snack will take center stage, and the urgency to leave will fade away.

It's all about recognizing when the current conversation or situation is going nowhere and finding a softer, more enjoyable path to take instead.

The Art of Agreement: "You're Absolutely Right"

There will be times when, no matter what you say, your loved one is stuck on an idea that isn't quite based in reality. Maybe they think they need to get to work, even though they've been retired for years, or they're convinced someone is coming over when no one is. These moments can be stressful, but here's a little secret: you don't have to fight it.

Sometimes, the easiest way to redirect is by agreeing with them—at least enough to calm things down. Saying, "You're absolutely right, but first, let's do [insert calming activity]" can work wonders. The goal isn't to correct them; it's to guide them back to a place of calm.

For instance, if my dad thought he had an important appointment, I'd say, "You're right, Dad, we'll get ready to go in a bit. How about we have a banana while we wait?" By the time the banana was peeled and eaten, the urgency had usually passed. Problem solved.

Celebrate the Little Victories

If you manage to turn a moment of frustration into laughter or peace, that's a victory worth celebrating. Even the smallest success—whether it's distracting them with a snack or making them laugh with a silly joke—can feel like a huge win when you're navigating the ups and downs of dementia care.

Don't forget to give yourself credit for those moments. Redirecting someone from frustration to fun takes patience and creativity, and every time you manage to do it, you're making their day (and yours) just a little bit brighter.

At the end of the day, the art of the gentle redirect is really about love and patience. It's about meeting your loved one where they are and helping them find their way back to a calmer, happier space. Sometimes it's a laugh, sometimes it's a snack, sometimes it's just a peaceful moment together. And that's the magic—taking something hard and making it a little easier, a little lighter, and a little more joyful.

So next time things start getting tense, think of yourself as a magician, gently redirecting the energy in the room. Whether it's with a snack, a joke, or a simple change of subject, you have the power to turn frustration into fun. And when you can do that, you're creating moments of peace and joy for both of you.

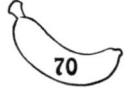

Helpful Tip # 15
Animal Medicine: The Magic of Pets

Most days, when I visited my dad, I'd bring along my two dogs, Finnley and Giggles. And honestly, seeing how much joy they brought him was something I'll never forget. He'd sit there, banana in one hand and his other hand resting on one of the dogs, totally in his element. Finnley was my first dog, and Dad was so familiar with her; they had a bond that went back years. But when Finnley had puppies, things got even better.

I remember bringing him over to my house to visit the puppies, and it was like seeing a spark of his old self come to life. He was completely enamored with them, watching them tumble around, and he couldn't get enough. Giggles, the first-born pup I kept, became another source of comfort for him. Finnley and Giggles together—they were like little bundles of love, a kind of therapy that words can't quite capture. And the way they nuzzled up to him, how he'd light up every time they were around—it was something so pure, so simple, and so healing.

I'll never forget the day when the puppies were about six weeks old. The memory care facility let me bring all eight of them to the secured courtyard. You can't imagine the scene—eight tiny pups running wild, the residents just sitting there, wide-eyed and grinning from ear to ear. Some of them even held the puppies in their laps, and for a little while, the whole place was filled with nothing but laughter and joy. It was like the entire atmosphere transformed. The happiness those pups spread that day—well, it's hard to put into words, but you could feel it in the air. Dog medicine is real, and those little furballs proved it.

And it wasn't just dogs that brought him joy. When my dad would visit my sister, he was equally enamored with her cats. They had this beautiful, calming effect on him. The cats would curl up on his lap, purring away as they sat together, sharing stories, singing, and even yodeling. My sister had this incredible way of making him feel welcome and at home. Watching them together, it was easy to see how much those moments meant to him. Cat love is different from dog love, but both are a tonic for the soul. Whether it's a purring feline or a wagging tail, the comfort animals provide is unlike anything else.

Pets, especially ones your loved one already knows and loves, have this magical way of breaking through the fog of dementia. They bring out something that often feels lost—joy, comfort, a sense of connection. Even if your loved one doesn't remember the pet's name or specific memories, there's this deeper recognition that happens. It's not about the details; it's about the feeling they get—the love that pets offer without any expectations.

If the memory care facility allows it, I can't recommend enough bringing your family pet for visits. Whether it's a dog, a cat, or even a gentle bunny, there's something about animals that can calm the mind and lift the spirit in ways that go beyond words. It's like bringing a little piece of home to your loved one, wrapped up in fur and unconditional love.

In a reality that can feel confusing and overwhelming for someone with dementia, pets have this beautiful way of reminding us that comfort, joy, and connection are still very much alive. Even if the interaction only lasts a few minutes, the calm and happiness they bring can linger long after the visit is over. It's a small thing, really, but the impact it has—it's everything.

Helpful Tip # 16
Capture those Banana Moments

You know that smartphone that's in your pocket, don't let it sit idle. Start snapping those photos and taking those videos now. You're not just capturing moments; you're preserving *banana moments*—the funny, sweet, sometimes random flashes of joy that make your loved one who they are. Think of these photos and videos as mementos of the little things you'll cherish later, long after the conversations have slipped away. Organize them into folders and tags for easy recall. One day, you'll look back and laugh at how your dad peeled banana after banana like he'd never seen one before or how your mom cracked up at a joke she'd heard a hundred times. These moments might seem ordinary now, but just like a banana turning from green to perfectly ripe, they'll become more precious with time.

One day, you'll realize that the photos and videos you took aren't just images—they're pieces of a story that will live on. A story filled with love, laughter, and all the moments that made your time together special. When dementia starts stealing those little day-to-day memories, that's when these captured moments become invaluable. A snapshot of your dad in the middle of his banana-peeling spree or a video of your mom slipping into fits of giggles over something silly—these will be your treasures. So don't wait for the "perfect" moment; grab your phone or camera and start collecting these moments before they ripen and pass.

I know this personally. Over the final five years of my dad's life, I captured hundreds of short videos on my iPhone during our visits. Every clip, every laugh, every quiet moment—it's all there. And now, when I look at those videos, it's as if he's still alive. I get to enjoy the memory of him, the way his smile lit up the room, or how he would joyfully eat his bananas. But now, I can enjoy these memories without the responsibility of caregiving. These videos are more than just recordings; they're living pieces of his spirit, and watching them brings me comfort and joy long after he's gone.

The Power of the Everyday Moment

You might think, "Why bother taking a picture? We're just sitting here." But those are exactly the moments that will mean the most to you later. A candid shot of your mom laughing over lunch or a quick video of your dad singing his favorite song—these are the bits of life that show who they truly are, even as dementia weaves its way through your conversations.

One day, you'll scroll through those photos and smile. You won't just see the dementia—you'll see *them*—the moments when they were fully present, fully alive, and full of personality. So, instead of waiting for something "special" to happen, capture the everyday banana moments because those little slices of joy are exactly what you'll want to remember.

Encouraging Stories That Connect Them to Their Past

Most people with dementia remember their early past more vividly than recent events. So, get proactive during your visits and encourage them to tell stories from way back when. Ask about their childhood, first car, or favorite holiday, and watch as they light up with memories. When you get them talking about the "good old days," you're helping them reconnect with the ripe moments of their life, the ones that shaped them.

And here's the fun part: record it. Take a video of your dad as he talks about the first banana he ever ate (who knew it could be such a monumental moment?) or snap a picture of your mom's delighted face as she describes her childhood. These aren't just stories—they're part of their legacy. When you revisit these memories later, you'll not only have their words but the joy on their face and the sound of their laughter. These moments will remind you that they were still very much themselves, even as dementia slipped in and peeled away the details.

The Unexpected Gifts of Video

Photos are great, but videos? They're golden. There's something magical about watching a video of your loved one—it's like pressing play on a memory that you can relive whenever you want. Hearing their voice, seeing them laugh, and catching their unique mannerisms brings them back to life in a way nothing else can. It's like biting into a perfectly ripe banana—sweet, satisfying, and something you didn't realize you craved until you had it again.

So go ahead—record the little chats, the silly dances, or the way they hum along to their favorite tune. Maybe your mom still tells the same story about how she snuck a banana split before dinner as a kid. Record it. Maybe your dad pretends to slip on an imaginary banana peel just to get a laugh. Record it. These are the banana moments you'll want to watch again and again.

Dignity in Every Frame

Dementia can feel like it snags away pieces of your loved one—but capturing them in their best moments reminds you of their dignity.

No matter what, they are still the person you've always known, who brought you into this world—full of quirks, love, and personality.

Let's be real—dementia can be hard. But when you look at those photos and videos later, it's the humor, the love, and the grace that will stand out. You'll remember the time your dad did something outrageous just to make you laugh, or the time your mom burst into laughter at a joke she didn't quite get but loved anyway.

The point isn't to capture picture-perfect moments—it's to capture the real ones. The banana-peeling, joke-telling, story-sharing moments that will fill your heart when you need them most. These are the moments where love and grace shine through, no matter how tough the road ahead may be.

The Lasting Legacy

When your loved one passes, the photos and videos you took will become part of their lasting legacy. It's not just about remembering who they were before dementia; it's about honoring who they were during their memory loss journey. Dementia might have peeled away parts of their memory, but it didn't take away their spirit, their joy, or the love they had for you.

Looking back at these banana-filled moments, you'll feel proud that you helped them live their final years with dignity and laughter. Proud that even through the tough times, you found ways to share love and joy. And you'll know that you didn't just care for them—you truly cherished them.

So, capture the moments: the smiles, the laughs, the quiet moments. Record their voice, their stories, their laughter. One day, you'll be glad you did. When words alone can't comfort you, those photos and videos will remind you that love, laughter, and grace were present, even on the hardest days. And they'll forever remind you that you gave them the best gift you could—the gift of a life lived with love, humor, dignity, and grace.

Helpful Tip # 17
BIG Love for the Unsung Heroes

Here's a priceless insight that will pay big dividends. Every time you visit your loved one, take a moment to appreciate the care team. These folks spend their days making sure your loved one is comfortable, safe, and cared for. A simple "hello" can work wonders. These caregivers are the hands that never stop peeling back the hard layers, keeping things running smoothly, even when the going gets tough. They deserve more than just a glance—they deserve genuine, heartfelt thanks for the beautiful work they do.

Let's be real for a second: the care staff at assisted living and memory care facilities are juggling more than just daily routines. They're handling unique personalities, family dynamics, and, let's face it, sometimes a bit of family drama (okay, maybe a lot). It's like keeping a bunch of

bananas from bruising—delicate work done with grace, compassion, and quiet strength. Showing a little gratitude can go a long way.

Maybe it's as simple as saying, "Thank you for everything you do," or bringing a small gesture, like a bouquet of flowers or a basket of snacks. It's the banana split of kindness—it shows them you see their effort, value their hard work, and appreciate the love they pour into caring for your loved one. These folks work long hours, peeling back emotional and physical exhaustion day after day. A small token, no matter how simple, can be a reminder that they are seen, valued, and appreciated.

It's not just about the physical gift—it's the thought behind it. You're recognizing their hard work, their compassion, and the vital role they play in your loved one's life. You're saying, "I see you, and I appreciate all you do." That little burst of gratitude can bring a smile to their faces and lift their spirits.

Build Bonds with the Care Team

Getting to know the care team on a personal level is one of the best things you can do. Ask about their lives and their interests. When you take the time to connect with them, it becomes more than just a transactional relationship. They're no longer just there to "do a job"— they become an extension of the support system for your loved one.

These caregivers are the ones who will be there when you can't be. They'll hold your loved one's hand during tough moments, sit with them when they feel confused or anxious, and offer comfort when needed. Building that connection creates trust, and you'll feel more at ease knowing your loved one is in good hands.

Holiday Love: Peel Some Extra Gratitude

The holidays are the perfect time to go the extra mile and show some love and gratitude, and what better way to start than with a little Halloween fun? Caregivers sacrifice their own time with family to care for your loved one, and that deserves some spooky recognition! Bring in some playful Halloween treats or fun decorations for the caregiver station. It's a lighthearted way to say, "I see you, and I appreciate the tricks and treats you bring to the lives of your residents every day!"

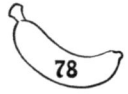

As the holidays roll on, don't forget about the rest—festive goodies for Christmas or Chanukkah or a special treat on New Year's. It could be something as simple as a box of holiday cookies or sparkling cider to ring in the new year with gratitude. Even small touches like these can brighten their day like a surprise Halloween banana treat.

And if you can't be there in person, no worries! You can still spread the holiday cheer by ordering gifts online. Imagine their surprise when a spooky Halloween gift arrives or a winter bouquet, reminding them that you appreciate their hard work. It's not about the size of the gift—it's about the thought behind it. You're peeling back the layers of the holiday hustle to show you care. And trust me, whether it's a spooky banana Halloween surprise or a cozy winter treat, that effort never goes unnoticed.

Handling those Slippery, Tough Days

There will be days when emotions run high, confusion turns to frustration, and things get tough. The care team is there to handle those moments with patience and grace—all day long. They bring calm to the storm, providing comfort when needed most. It's easy to forget how much emotional labor goes into this work, so take a moment to thank them for handling those tough days. Let them know you appreciate their calm, their compassion, and their ability to bring your loved one back to a place of peace.

Why Gratitude Matters: It's the Sweetness Inside

When caregivers feel appreciated, it shows in their work. They're more likely to communicate openly with you, sharing those small, joyful moments that happen when you're not around. Caregiving isn't just a job for these folks—it's a calling, much like peeling a banana to get to the sweetness inside. And when you express gratitude, it strengthens the relationship, making them feel seen for the incredibly hard work they do.

So, next time you visit, bring a little banana love. Share a kind word, a small gift, or simply a smile. Let the care team know their work matters—not just to your loved one, but to you. Because, in the end, it's about creating a circle of care. You, the caregivers, and your loved one—each part of that circle is essential, like a perfect bunch of bananas. Together, you create something sweet, nourishing, and full of love.

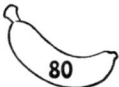

Helpful Tip # 18
When Family Doesn't Show Up

A ccepting "What Is…"

Let's talk about something that's not always easy to admit: Not everyone in your family will show up to help, and let me tell you, that can be one of the most frustrating parts of this whole caregiving journey. You might find yourself looking around, wondering where everyone else is. Why aren't they stepping in? Don't they realize what's happening? It's like you're juggling ten bananas, and everyone else is just sitting back, not even offering to peel one.

Naturally, you would think that when a loved one needs care, everyone will rally together, shoulder to shoulder, ready to support each other through the tough times. But reality doesn't always look like that perfect picture. In fact, caregiving can sometimes feel like you're holding the banana split together with one hand while the rest of the family is off enjoying dessert somewhere else.

The Weight of Expectations

It's completely normal to feel frustrated when family members don't show up the way you expect them to. You might find yourself thinking, *Shouldn't they care as much as I do?* or *Why am I the only one stepping up?* These thoughts can spiral into resentment, and that's where things get messy.

But here's the thing: people have their own ways of dealing (or not dealing) with difficult situations. Some people simply can't handle the emotional weight of caregiving, while others may be grappling with their own guilt, fear, or personal struggles. Accepting that everyone has different capacities can help ease the frustration, even if it doesn't completely take it away.

It's a tough pill to swallow, but here's the reality: not everyone is going to show up the way you need them to. Some might be physically absent; others might be emotionally distant. Some may not show up at all, and that can hurt—especially when you're the one in the trenches, doing the day-to-day caregiving.

But here's where a little grace comes in—for yourself and for them. Instead of focusing on what others aren't doing, try to focus on what *you* are doing. You're showing up. You're caring. You're making a difference in your loved one's life. Let that be enough. Let that be the part you hold onto, even when it feels like you're carrying more than your fair share of the load.

Acceptance doesn't mean you're okay with their absence, but it does mean that you're not letting it control your emotions or actions. It's about releasing that grip of expectation and finding peace in what *is,* not what you think should be.

For five long years, it was just my sister and I holding down the fort. While others faded into the background, she showed up in a big way—taking charge of photos and creating beautiful scrapbooks that captured those special moments. She picked out songs that made the hard days a little lighter and hand-crafted gifts with so much love that

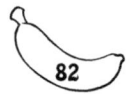

you could practically feel it radiating off of them. My sister literally poured her heart into everything she did, and it was a saving grace for our dad. I had my role, too, and together, we were the *Dad Love Team*.

But here's the thing: my sister and I couldn't change the fact that other family members didn't step in. What we could do was accept it and, in doing so, find peace. I know how frustrating it can be to feel like you're the only one carrying the load. It's hard not to resent the people who should be there and aren't—but holding onto that resentment? It's like holding onto a banana that's way past its prime—nothing good comes from it.

Setting Boundaries and Letting Go

If you're the one doing most (or all) of the caregiving, it's easy to feel like you have to be the rock all the time. But you don't. You're allowed to set boundaries, to say no when things get overwhelming, and to protect your own well-being.

And when it comes to family members who don't step up, sometimes it's helpful to have an honest conversation—not with an accusatory tone, but from a place of expressing your feelings and needs. Let them know how much it would mean to have their support, but also be prepared to let go of the outcome. If they still don't show up, at least you've done your part by communicating openly.

Beware of the Slippery Peel of Resentment

Resentment is one of those sneaky emotions that can creep up on you, especially when you're deep in the trenches of caregiving. It's like carrying a bunch of overripe bananas around—sticky, messy, and making everything feel harder than it already is. The longer you hold onto it, the more it starts to weigh you down, adding unnecessary stress to an already challenging situation.

So, how do you let go of that resentment? First, recognize that other people's absence or lack of involvement has nothing to do with your worth. It doesn't mean that you're not doing enough or that your loved one is any less deserving of care. It's about them—their choices, their ability (or inability) to step up—and not a reflection on you.

Letting go of resentment doesn't mean you have to be okay with how things are. It simply means you're choosing not to carry that emotional baggage around anymore. You're releasing the weight of expecting others to show up in ways they may never be able to, and instead, you're focusing on the love, care, and energy you're putting into your loved one's life. By letting go, you're giving yourself permission to focus on what really matters—your well-being and the connection you have with your loved one, without the burden of resentment slowing you down.

Lean on Your Caregiving Circle

While some family members may not show up, others might surprise you by stepping in. Friends, neighbors, and even members of the care team can become part of your caregiving circle. It might not look like the family team you expected, but it's still a team. Lean on them. Allow others to support you, even if they're not family by blood.

There are plenty of community volunteers who love being a friend to people with memory loss; churches, synagogues, senior centers, and local nonprofits have programs where volunteers dedicate their time to visiting or assisting those in need. These individuals can bring a fresh sense of connection, engaging your loved one in meaningful conversations, music, or simply sharing quiet moments.

It might not look like the family team you expected, but it's still a team full of people who genuinely care. Lean on them. Allow others to support you, even if they're not family by blood. The care and friendship they provide can be just as meaningful—sometimes even more so—because they've chosen to be there out of the goodness of their hearts.

You're not alone, even when it feels like it. There are people out there who understand the caregiving journey and are willing to help, even in small ways. Accept their support with open arms and know that it's okay to ask for help outside of your immediate family. It takes a village, and your village is out there—you just have to let them in.

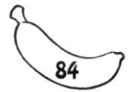

Shifting Your Focus

At the end of the day, caregiving isn't about who didn't show up. It's about your loved one and the love you're pouring into them, day after day. It's about the moments of connection, the small victories, and the care you're giving from your heart. Yes, it's hard when others don't step up, but try not to let that define your experience. Shift your focus to the present moment, to the good you're doing, and to the love that's guiding you. You're making a difference in someone's life, and that's what matters most.

It's okay to feel frustrated when family doesn't show up. It's okay to feel disappointed. But remember, you're doing something incredible—something that not everyone is capable of. You're showing up. You're caring. And you're making a difference, even when it feels like you're going at it alone. Accept what is, allow others to be who they are, and give yourself credit for the amazing work you're doing.

Yes, being actively involved in the care of my dad for five years took a big chunk out of my time to do other things for myself. There were moments when I felt stretched thin, wondering if I'd ever have time for my own life again. But now that he has passed, when I look at all the pictures and videos, it was worth it. Every smile, every laugh, every shared moment—it's all there, captured in those memories, reminding me that those years were about love, about showing up when it mattered most.

Thank you for being here, for showing up in your caregiving journey, and for allowing yourself to embrace the ups, downs, and everything in between. You're not just a caregiver—you're a superhero. And that's something to be proud of.

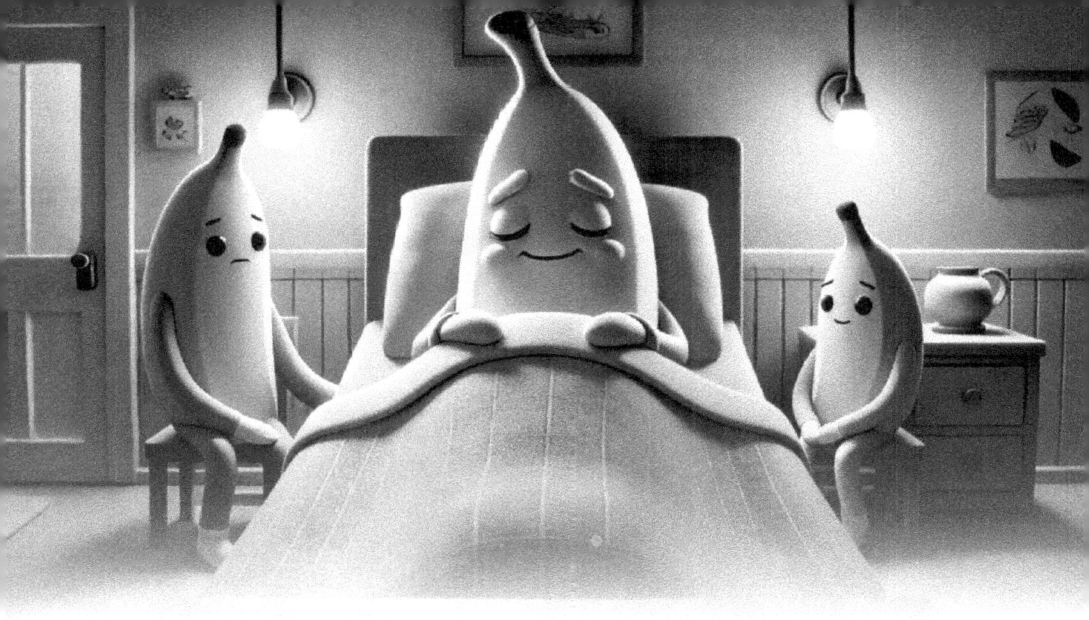

The Last Banana

Wu hen the call came that our dad was getting ready to transition, my sister and I rushed to the memory care facility, hearts pounding, unsure of what we would find. He was moved to the "Family Room"—the room where people are taken to die. Sitting in that sterile, quiet space, we both felt the weight of the moment, the reality of what was happening, but something didn't sit right. This wasn't where his story was supposed to end. Not in this room.

Our dad lived too large of a life for that. He was a wild card of a man, the kind who didn't just live—he thrived. A world traveler, cyclist, camper, skier, mountain climber, real estate broker, electrical engineer, auctioneer, art collector, and, of course, a dad. His spirit couldn't be confined to a place like the Family Room.

I thought back to those days in the 1960s and 70s when my sister and I would ride in the child seats on the back of his bicycle as he whirled us around Central Park, yodeling as we sped through the air, our laughter ringing out with his melodies. He loved that bicycle. He rode the same one for over 50 years, and it became a symbol of his

adventurous, carefree soul. He was always on the move, always finding new ways to embrace life. He lived under the sun, shirtless whenever he could be, proudly showing off his physique, the result of a lifetime dedicated to bodybuilding. Even with dementia, he kept riding that bike, lifting weights, and staying fit up until the age of 92 when he finally had a stroke that began the winding down of his life's story.

No, the Family Room was not where his story would end. This was a man who lived under open skies, who thrived in nature, and who found joy in the warmth of the sun on his skin. My sister and I knew what we had to do. We asked if we could roll his bed outside, into the courtyard, under the clear blue sky, and they agreed.

We took off his shirt, just like he always did when he felt the sun's rays, and we let him spend his final unconscious hours as he had spent so many in his life—shirtless, basking in the sun. The moment felt right. This was his true farewell, not enclosed by walls but under the vast, open sky that he loved so much.

The warmth of the sun kissed his skin, the same sun he chased on countless adventures—skiing down mountains, climbing peaks, cycling through parks, camping in the wilderness, and building a life filled with bold, unapologetic joy. As we sat beside him, my sister and I felt at peace. It was as if we returned him to where he belonged. The sun, the sky, the open air—that was his true family room.

In those final moments, we knew we weren't just saying goodbye. We were honoring the man he had always been and letting him transition with the dignity he deserved in a space that was as big and full of life as he was.

He was more than the illness that had taken him into this slow goodbye. He was all the things that made him vibrant and unique: the auctioneer's voice that never wavered, the cyclist who rode until the very end, the proud bodybuilder who never shied away from taking his shirt off to soak in the sun. His story didn't end in a quiet room where people go to pass away. It ended under the same open sky where he lived his life to the fullest.

In those last hours, the sun shone down, his skin warm to the touch, and the sky stretched above us, as wide and limitless as his spirit had always been. We wanted to make sure his final moments were filled with everything he loved. We draped him with photos of his favorite memories—pictures of all his children and a copy of *Hibble Pibble and Zibble*, the children's book he wrote in 1964 about three adventurous frogs, which I published for his 92nd birthday, and it became his most cherished keepsake during his final years. He kept it nearby all the time and read it over and over like it was the greatest prize life had given him.

We sat there, talking to him as if he were still listening, playing his favorite music, telling him stories, and reminding him how much we loved him. We spoke about his favorite things—his bike rides through Central Park, his yodeling, his days as an auctioneer, and how he always went shirtless in the sun, proud of his body. And yes, we placed a banana in his hands throughout the day and night because that felt right. It was a small comfort, a piece of him, just as familiar as anything else in those final hours.

When he finally exhaled his last breath at 5:15 p.m., after five hours of lying under the sun, we sat there with him, watching as the pulse in his neck slowed down to nothing. We held his hands, tears falling, whispering words of love as he made his final transition. The sun was still warm on his skin, and somehow, that brought us peace. This was the perfect ending for a man who lived so much of his life outdoors, in the sunlight, shirtless, enjoying every minute of it.

When the staff came, eager to take his body away, we asked them, "What's the rush?" He was gone, yes, but there was no reason to hurry. No one had ever kept their parent outside after they passed, but for us, it felt right. So, we stayed with him under the stars until after 9 p.m., talking to him, sharing more stories, and helping him transition in our own way. We imagined him making his way to *Glocca Morra*, his favorite place from the song, which brought him so much joy.

When it was finally time, we buried him in Telluride, Colorado, with a view of the most beautiful Box Canyon in the world. We placed a memory box beside him, filled with photos of his life, pictures of his children, and, of course, his beloved *Hibble Pibble and Zibble*. And now, when we visit him, we don't bring flowers—we bring bananas because that's how we keep his spirit alive.

One day, I was talking to the cemetery groundskeeper, and he mentioned that there always seemed to be chipmunks around my dad's grave. I laughed and told him, "It's probably from the bananas." I shared the story with him, and we both chuckled, imagining the little critters enjoying the bananas we left, just like Dad would have.

In the end, this wasn't just about how he left us—it was about how we kept him with us. His story didn't end in some quiet room. It ended under the sun, under the stars, surrounded by the love of his family and the things that made him who he was. And yes, with a banana in his hand. That's how it was always meant to be.

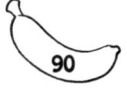

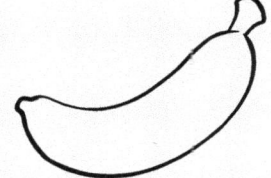

Part Two

Peeling it All Together

A Whole Bunch of Bananas

S o, here we are! You've reached the end of *The Heartfelt Handbook for Caregivers*, and what a banana-flavored adventure it's been! If you've made it this far, you're practically a caregiving superhero—fully equipped with all the tips, tricks, and banana peels of wisdom you need to navigate this wild, heartwarming, and sometimes downright challenging world of caring for your loved one. Let's peel back the core takeaways from our journey.

Gratitude Goes a Long Way

Whether it's saying a quick hello to the care team or leaving a little treat, we've learned that small gestures of gratitude can make a big impact. Remember, showing appreciation doesn't have to be grand—it's all about the thought behind it. A "thank you" is like giving someone an unexpected banana split: sweet, simple, and oh-so-rewarding.

Build Your Care Team Relationships

Caregiving isn't just about your loved one—it's about the relationships you build with the people who help you along the way. Caregivers are human, not robots (though that might make things interesting!). A simple connection goes a long way, so keep those banana bread batches and thank-you notes flowing, and don't be shy about showing some love.

Celebrate the Small Wins

A box of chocolates, a thank-you note, or even a bouquet of flowers left at the caregiver station—these are the little gestures that brighten someone's day, even on the roughest shifts. Celebrate the small victories, whether it's your loved one having a great day or you lifting a caregiver's spirits with some spooky Halloween bananas. Those little moments add up.

Embrace the Tough Days with Grace (and Humor)

We didn't sugarcoat it—there will be tough days. But here's the thing: tough days don't last; tough people do. When you're in the thick of it, remember that grace and humor are your best allies. When life gives you overripe bananas, make banana bread—and don't forget the chocolate chips for a little extra sweetness.

Keep Your Heart Open

At the heart of it all, this journey is about love. It's about showing up for your loved one, for yourself, and for the amazing caregivers who are part of the story. Keep your heart open, spread kindness, and always share the banana-flavored love.

Remember to Have Fun

Caregiving can be stressful, but don't forget to laugh, play, and enjoy the silly moments. Life's too short to be serious all the time, so whether you're pulling pranks with the care team or sneaking in a banana-themed gift, make room for fun. The lighthearted moments are just as meaningful as the serious ones—they keep us grounded in love and joy.

So, as you move forward in your caregiving journey, take a deep breath, savor the ride, and never underestimate the power of a good banana. You've got this, superhero! Thanks for joining me on this journey, and may your caregiving days be filled with love, laughter, and plenty of bananas.

Taking Care of Them Means Taking Care of You

O ne last thing. I know how it goes. You're running yourself ragged, trying to make sure your loved one has everything they need, all while your own needs get pushed to the back burner. It's so easy to get caught up in being the "superhero caregiver," thinking if you're not there 24/7, you're somehow failing them. Trust me, I've been there. But here's something I learned the hard way: you can't care for them properly if you're running on empty.

Being a caregiver, especially for someone with dementia, is no small thing. It's a full-time job with no clock-out button. And the truth is, it takes a toll—physically, mentally, emotionally. The stress builds, and before you know it, you're exhausted, snapping at people for little things or maybe even crying in the car before you go inside. I'm here to tell you *it's okay to feel that way.*

The Caregiver Guilt Trap

I can't tell you how many times I felt guilty for thinking, "I just need a break." You feel bad for wanting some time to yourself, like you're being selfish for wanting to take a nap or watch a TV show without being interrupted. But here's the deal: self-care isn't selfish. In fact, it's one of the best things you can do—not just for you, but for them.

Taking care of someone is draining, and it's easy to lose yourself in it. You might feel like if you're not there every second, something will go wrong. But if you don't take care of yourself, how are you supposed to keep showing up for them? You need to refill your own cup. And yes, that might mean taking a step back, letting someone else take over for a bit, or just doing something small that brings *you* joy.

Find Little Moments for Yourself. Maybe it's a walk around the block, a few minutes to read a book, or even just sitting quietly with a cup of tea. Whatever it is, *do it*. Give yourself permission. You can't be on call 24/7 and still expect to be your best self. It's okay to say, "I need a breather." It's okay to set boundaries. Heck, it's necessary. I remember feeling like I had to be the rock, holding everything together, but even rocks wear down over time.

Dignity for Them, Dignity for You

Here's the thing: caring for someone with dementia is about helping them live their final years with dignity. But you know what? *You deserve dignity, too.* You're not a machine, and caregiving doesn't mean you have to sacrifice your own well-being. It's about harmony. They need you, but you also need *you*. It's okay to take care of yourself because when you're feeling more centered and cared for, that's when you can give the best care.

And let's be real—this journey isn't easy. There are tough days when it feels like nothing is going right, and it's easy to feel alone in it all. But taking a step back doesn't mean you're abandoning them. It means you're being smart about how you show up. You need those moments of rest to recharge so you can come back with more energy, more patience, and more love.

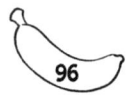

Give Yourself Some Grace

It's okay to admit that this is hard. It's okay to feel frustrated. And it's okay to ask for help. You don't have to do it all, even though it can feel like that sometimes. Lean on others when you need to. Caregiving isn't about being perfect; it's about being *present*. And the only way you can truly be present is by making sure *you* are taken care of, too.

So yeah, give yourself some grace. You're doing something incredible, even if it doesn't always feel like it. And just remember—taking care of yourself is part of the journey. It's not an "extra." It's how you keep going, and it's how you give your loved one the care and love they deserve.

You've got this, but you're allowed to rest.

Part Three

Before and After Transitions

Preparing for the Early Stages of Memory Loss

When you start to notice the early signs of memory loss in your loved one, it can feel overwhelming—but this is actually the perfect time to get a head start on planning for the long, slippery road ahead. Before dementia fully takes hold, this is your golden opportunity to take inventory of the things that make them who they are: their favorite memories, foods they love, hobbies that bring them joy, and even the little quirks that light them up. Trust me, this groundwork will be a lifesaver later on.

Start with the basics. What are the stories they've always loved telling? What songs make them tap their toes or bring a smile to their face? Are there any comfort foods that have been staples throughout their life? If your loved one has favorite books, movies, or hobbies, now's the time to make note of them. These details will be your treasure trove when they can no longer communicate as easily. And the best part? It gives you a way to connect with them even when their memory starts to fade.

Don't just think of it as preparation—think of it as preserving their legacy. You're gathering up the pieces that make up their story, and you'll be able to use those pieces to create moments of joy and familiarity down the road. Even something as simple as knowing they love chocolate chip cookies, or their morning cup of tea can be a comfort when the future feels uncertain.

Take the time to capture their essence now. Have conversations, ask questions, and be curious about the details of their life. If they're still able, involve them in the process. Maybe even make a little memory book together. What's their favorite holiday tradition? Who was their childhood best friend? What's their favorite way to spend a lazy afternoon?

By preparing in these early stages, you're setting yourself—and your loved one—up for a smoother transition into memory care. You'll have a toolkit of things to pull from when the road gets tough, and it'll help you navigate the ups and downs with a little more grace and a lot more love. After all, this journey isn't just about managing memory loss—it's about keeping their spirit alive, one cherished memory at a time.

Early-Stage Memory Loss Checklist

1. **Favorite Memories**
- Identify stories they've always loved telling.
- Record or write down special moments from their life that bring them joy.
- Create videos of them sharing their favorite stories—these can be a comfort later on.

2. **Music That Moves Them**
- Make a note of songs or albums that make them smile, tap their toes, or feel at peace.
- Create a personalized playlist for future moments when music can calm or uplift them.

3. Comfort Foods

Write down their favorite comfort foods and drinks, like a beloved recipe or a daily ritual, such as their morning cup of tea or chocolate chip cookies.

Try to keep a supply of these favorites on hand to help ground them in moments of confusion.

1. Hobbies and Activities

- Take stock of the activities they've always enjoyed, such as reading, knitting, gardening, or watching certain movies.

- Consider ways to simplify these hobbies to make them accessible in later stages.

2. Quirks and Preferences

- Identify the little quirks that bring them happiness. Do they love a certain chair, a favorite sweater, or a particular morning routine?

- These personal details will help maintain a sense of familiarity and comfort.

3. Favorite Books, Movies, and TV Shows

- Make a list of their go-to entertainment—books they've read repeatedly or movies they never get tired of watching.

- Prepare a collection for future enjoyment when other forms of engagement may become difficult.

4. Legacy Conversations

- Ask about their favorite holiday traditions, childhood memories, or the people who've meant the most to them.

- Consider creating a memory book together filled with photos, stories, and mementos.

5. Spiritual Practices

- Take note of any religious or spiritual practices that bring them peace, such as prayer, meditation, or attending services.

- Keep these practices part of their routine as memory loss progresses.

6. **Capture Essence with Videos and Photos**

- Take the time to film or photograph them during happy moments, capturing their essence.

- Record conversations where they talk about their life, memories, and experiences. These videos will be invaluable later.

Preparing for memory loss doesn't have to feel overwhelming. By focusing on the little details—their favorite foods, cherished stories, beloved music—you're preserving the essence of who they are. These memories and preferences will help you create moments of joy and comfort as their journey with dementia unfolds. It's not just about planning ahead; it's about ensuring that even as their memory fades, their spirit shines brightly through the love and care you provide. You're not just preparing for the hard times—you're laying the foundation for continued connection, grace, and joy.

Life at Home with Memory Loss

Whe your loved one with memory loss is still living at home or comes to visit, it can be a mixed bag of emotions. On one hand, it's comforting to have them in familiar surroundings. On the other hand, there are challenges—forgetting where things are, asking the same questions, and getting confused by even the simplest things. It can be a lot to handle, but with some thoughtful planning and a whole lot of love, you can make these moments smoother for both of you.

Keeping Things Familiar and Safe

First things first—whether they're living with you, visiting, or still in their own home, creating a space that feels both familiar and safe is key. You want them to feel comfortable but also avoid confusion or frustration.

- **Consistency is Everything**: Try to keep their everyday essentials like glasses, keys, or a favorite blanket in the same spot. Familiarity helps them navigate their space without feeling lost.

- **Label It Up**: Adding simple labels to drawers, cabinets, or even doors can be a game changer. A photo or a word can offer that extra bit of guidance without them needing to ask where things are.

- **Declutter the Space**: A tidy environment reduces confusion. Keeping pathways clear and surfaces uncluttered can help them avoid frustration. Plus, a clean space is more peaceful for everyone.

The Power of Routine

Routine is your best friend when it comes to memory loss. Predictability brings comfort, giving your loved one a sense of control in an otherwise confusing world.

- **Stick to a Schedule**: Regular meal times, activities, and naps provide structure. It's not about packing the day full but about giving it some rhythm. That kind of consistency is calming for everyone.

- **Avoid Overstimulation**: Keep activities simple and allow for plenty of downtime. Too much at once can be overwhelming. If things start to feel hectic, it's okay to hit pause and switch to something quieter.

Handling Repetition Like a Pro

Ah, repetition—the same questions, the same stories, over and over. It's one of the toughest parts of memory loss. But here's the thing: for them, it's new every time.

- **Answer Like it's the First Time**: Even if you've heard the same question five times in ten minutes, try to respond with patience. They're not trying to wear you out; they just can't remember. Your calm reaction will help keep them calm, too.

- **Gently Shift the Conversation**: If they're stuck in a loop, try offering a distraction. Bring them a snack, suggest a walk, or ask them about something they enjoy. Sometimes, a gentle nudge in a different direction can help reset the mood.

Make Every Visit Special

Whether they're living with you or just visiting, it's the little things that can make a huge difference. Even with memory loss, you can create moments that are joyful and meaningful.

- **Bring Their Favorite Treat**: Something as simple as a fresh batch of cookies or their favorite fruit can bring comfort and familiarity. Those small gestures go a long way in brightening their day.

- **Do Something Familiar Together**: If they once loved gardening, knitting, or watching classic movies, revisit those activities. It's less about the task itself and more about sharing a moment they can still connect with.

When Frustration Kicks In

Let's be real—there will be frustrating moments. Whether they're upset because they can't remember something or you're feeling overwhelmed from answering the same question for the tenth time, emotions will run high. The trick is to approach these moments with as much patience and grace as you can.

- **Stay Calm and Reassure Them**: When they're upset, remind them that everything's okay and you're there to help. They may not understand why they're frustrated, but your calmness can help ease the tension.

- **Take Breaks**: It's important to take care of yourself, too. If you're feeling overwhelmed, it's okay to step out for a moment and breathe. Caregiving is hard, and you deserve to recharge.

When Home is No Longer Safe

There may come a time when home just isn't the safest option for your loved one anymore. That's a tough reality to accept, but their safety and well-being come first. Before making any big decisions about memory care, take a step back and explore community resources that might help you bridge the gap. This preparation can buy you time, and it can make the eventual transition smoother for everyone involved.

Programs like Meals on Wheels are a fantastic resource, ensuring they're getting nutritious meals delivered right to their door. Religious organizations like churches and synagogues often offer emotional and spiritual support, social activities, and even caregiving help. Local municipal recreation centers or private organizations might provide adult day care, respite care, or support groups that can ease your load without jumping immediately to full-time memory care.

Have the Conversation Early

No one wants to leave the comfort of their home. So, when it's time to have that difficult conversation about moving to a memory care facility or bringing in more help, try to approach it with patience and compassion. Focus on how it will keep them safe and well cared for. Listen to their concerns and reassure them that this is all about making sure they feel supported and secure. It's not an easy conversation, but having it early gives everyone a chance to process, adjust, and be part of the decision-making process.

Cherishing Every Moment

Whether they're still living at home or visiting you, remember that these moments are fleeting, and there's beauty in each one. Even if things aren't like they used to be, there's still plenty of meaning in the time you spend together.

- **Be Present:** Whether it's watching TV, enjoying a meal, or just sitting in comfortable silence, be fully present. These small, quiet moments can become the memories you cherish most, so make an effort to savor them.

- **Capture the Joy:** Take pictures, record videos, and save the laughter. These will be your keepsakes, reminders of the love and joy that filled your journey together.

- **Celebrate the Little Wins:** Even if it's just a shared smile or a moment of calm, cherish it. These little victories are what make the hard days a little easier.

Look for Warning Signs

As time goes on, you may notice warning signs that indicate your loved one needs more structured care. Forgetting to turn off the stove, getting lost in familiar places, or wandering outside at unusual times—these are all signals that it might be time to explore other options for their safety and well-being. Be proactive in looking for these signs and trust your instincts.

Explore Community Resources

There are often local resources available that can provide support long before full-time memory care becomes necessary. Explore options like:

- **Meals on Wheels** to ensure they're eating well.
- **Churches, synagogues, and other religious groups** that offer emotional and caregiving support.
- **Adult daycare centers** that provide a break for caregivers and give your loved one a safe space to spend time outside the house.
- **Recreational programs** or local senior centers that offer activities and social engagement.
- **Private organizations** that provide respite care give you a chance to recharge.

Become Familiar with Costs and Assistance

Memory care can be expensive, so it's crucial to start planning ahead. Take the time to understand the costs associated with different types of care. Do they have the financial resources to cover these expenses? Are they eligible for government assistance like Medicaid or even local programs that provide financial support for seniors in need? Don't wait until it's too late—being proactive in financial planning can make a world of difference in reducing stress for both you and your loved one.

Take Advantage of Assistance Programs

Aside from government aid, look into final expense insurance and other forms of financial assistance that can help cover the cost of care. Having this safety net in place can offer peace of mind, knowing your loved one is financially secure, no matter what the future holds.

Cherish the Journey

As challenging as this journey can be, it's important to keep your attention on what really matters: spending time with your loved one and making sure they're safe and comfortable. While it's easy to get caught up in the planning and decisions, don't lose sight of the present moments. Whether it's a quick chat, sharing a meal, or just sitting quietly together, these are the moments that count.

Let the support systems around you do some of the heavy lifting. Community resources, daycare programs, and other forms of help are there for a reason—use them. They'll give you more breathing room to be present for your loved one without the extra stress.

Final Arrangements — Planning Ahead

When my dad passed away, I was completely caught off guard by how much I didn't know about handling final arrangements. I had been so focused on taking care of him that I never even thought about what would come next—the mortuary, the costs, burial vs. cremation, spiritual preferences. It was overwhelming to deal with all of this on top of the grief I was feeling. Looking back, I wish I had taken the time to plan for these things ahead of time instead of waiting until I was in the thick of it.

If you're caring for someone with dementia or a long-term illness, I really encourage you to start thinking about this now. I know it's not the easiest thing to talk about, but trust me, having a plan in place will make things so much smoother when the time comes.

So, here's what I would've done differently, and I hope it helps you prepare for what's to come:

1. Have the Hard Conversations Early

You probably don't want to talk about this stuff anymore than I did. But it's important to ask your loved one what their wishes are while they can still tell you. Do they want to be buried or cremated? What kind of memorial would they like? Would they prefer something religious, spiritual, or non-traditional? You'll feel so much more at peace knowing you're honoring their wishes when the time comes.

2. Burial vs. Cremation: Know the Options

When my dad passed, I had to figure out what made the most sense for us quickly. Here's a quick rundown to help you:

- **Burial**: This is often the more traditional route. It can be comforting to know there's a physical place where you can visit them, like a cemetery. But keep in mind, it tends to be more expensive with costs like the plot, casket, and headstone.

- **Cremation**: This is usually less expensive and offers flexibility. You can keep the ashes in an urn, scatter them somewhere meaningful, or even turn them into keepsakes. Cremation can still include a memorial service or celebration of life—there's no "one right way" to do it.

Knowing these options ahead of time and having your loved one's preference will take a lot of stress off your shoulders when the time comes.

3. Pick a Mortuary or Funeral Home in Advance

One thing I didn't expect was how quickly I had to decide on a funeral home after my dad passed. If I could go back, I'd research local mortuaries in advance, ask around for recommendations, and compare costs. Many places offer pre-planning services, which can help you have everything in place before you even need it.

4. Look Into Final Expense Insurance

Funerals are expensive—I learned this the hard way. Final expense insurance is something I wish I had known about. It's a small policy that covers funeral costs, burial or cremation, and other final expenses.

Even if your loved one doesn't already have this, it's something you can look into now. It can save you from scrambling later when you're already dealing with enough.

5. Start Thinking About the Memorial

This doesn't have to be a big, traditional funeral if that's not what you or your loved one wants. Maybe it's a celebration of life or something more personal and intimate. Think about who they would want to speak at the service, what music they'd like, or if there are any special readings or poems that are meaningful to them. These little details will make the service feel more like a tribute to their life and less like just a formality.

6. Get Their Documents in Order

I can't stress this enough—organize your loved one's important documents now. When the time comes, you'll need things like their birth certificate, Social Security number, will or trust documents, and any veteran's paperwork. I had to scramble to find these for my dad, and it made everything harder. Save yourself that stress and get these in order ahead of time.

7. Lean on Your Support System

I made the mistake of thinking I had to do everything myself. I didn't reach out to enough people for help, and looking back, I wish I had. Whether it's family, friends, or even a spiritual leader, don't be afraid to ask for help. They can help with the decision-making process or even just be there to listen when it all feels too much.

8. Plan for What Comes After the Funeral

It doesn't end after the service. There are still things to handle—like paying off final expenses, managing their estate, or handling their belongings. If your loved one doesn't have a will, this process can get complicated. Start thinking about who will handle these details now so you're not left figuring it out when you're already emotionally drained.

Planning for the final stages of life isn't something anyone looks forward to, but it's one of the greatest acts of love you can give to both your loved one and yourself. By taking the time now to think about their wishes, make important decisions, and get everything in order, you'll be giving yourself the gift of peace when the time comes. You won't have to navigate everything in the thick of grief—you'll already have a plan in place. And trust me, when the time comes, you'll be grateful for that foresight. Use this checklist as a guide, lean on your support system, and remember—you don't have to do it all alone.

Creating a Legacy

After my dad passed, it took me a few months to really process the loss. At first, it was all about the shock, grief, and trying to get through the daily motions of life without him. But about six months in, my mindset shifted. I began thinking in terms of legacy—how do I want my dad to be remembered? What stories do we want to share about him with future generations? This became a deeply meaningful part of my healing process, and it helped me focus on celebrating his life rather than just mourning his loss.

My sister and I started having a lot of conversations about this. Since we chose burial, we talked about what we wanted to write on his gravestone. It's such a small space, but you want it to say something that encapsulates who they were. It's not an easy decision, but it's important. We wanted something that spoke to his humor, his kindness, and the joy he brought to the world. The gravestone is a permanent reminder of his life, and we wanted to make sure it reflected him well.

Then there were the digital legacies—his Facebook page and Instagram account. These days, people have their entire lives documented online, and even though he's no longer here, those pages are still active. We had to decide whether to keep them up as a memorial or close them down. Between my sister and me, we had thousands of photos and videos of Dad, moments that capture his spirit, his laughter, and even some of his goofiest yodeling sessions. It felt powerful to look through these memories and decide how to share them with others.

Creating a legacy is a way to honor your loved one's life and ensure their memory lives on. There are so many options to consider:

1. Create a Memory Photo Book

One of the easiest things you can do is create a photo book for the family. Go through old albums, digital photos, and videos, selecting moments that represented their different stages of his life. It is a beautiful way to look back on their journey and bring recognition and closure that can be passed down to future generations, ensuring their story doesn't get lost over time.

2. Memorialize Social Media

If your loved one was active on social media, you might choose to turn their Facebook or Instagram into a memorial page. This way, friends and family can visit their profiles, leave messages, and share memories. It keeps their digital footprint alive in a respectful and heartfelt way. Or, if it feels right for you, you can close their accounts and preserve their memory in other forms.

3. Create a Digital Archive

With so many photos and videos on our phones, it's easy to forget how much we've captured over the years. Consider creating a digital archive of your loved one's life—organizing their photos, videos, and important documents into one place. It's a great way to ensure those memories don't get lost in the shuffle of everyday life. You can even create a website or blog dedicated to their life, where friends and family can share stories, pictures, and updates.

4. Make a Video Tribute

If you've got a treasure trove of videos, you can create a video tribute that showcases their life. It can be a mix of personal footage, favorite songs,

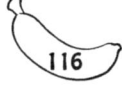

and meaningful quotes. This can be shared at a memorial service or family gathering or even just kept as a cherished keepsake for future generations.

5. Write Their Story

Another way to create a legacy is through storytelling. You can write a memoir about your loved one's life, capturing their adventures, quirks, and lessons. It doesn't have to be a professional book—it could be something as simple as a personal journal where you write down all the stories you don't want to forget. This can be passed down through the family and become a beautiful tribute to their life.

6. Celebrate Their Passions

Was your loved one passionate about something—music, art, sports, or a particular cause? You can honor their memory by creating a legacy project that reflects their passions. Maybe it's sponsoring an event in their name, creating a scholarship, or making a donation to a cause they care about. These are meaningful ways to keep their spirit alive and have their legacy impact others.

7. Gravestones and Memorials

The gravestone or memorial is another tangible way to leave a lasting mark. Think about what words, symbols, or quotes best represent your loved one's life. It's a small space, but those words will be there forever, so take your time in choosing something that feels right. You might even involve close family or friends in the decision-making process to make sure it feels like a fitting tribute.

8. Create a Website Memorial with a QR Code on the Gravestone

For a truly modern tribute, consider creating a website dedicated to your loved one's life. This site can house photos, videos, stories, and memories from friends and family. By placing a QR code on their gravestone, you invite visitors to access this digital memorial anytime they come to pay their respects. It allows loved ones to feel connected, reliving the moments that made your family member unique, and sharing memories that might otherwise be forgotten.

Creating a legacy for someone you love is a deeply personal and powerful experience. It's a way to make sure their life is remembered with love and meaning. For me, thinking about my dad's legacy helped turn my grief into a celebration of who he was. It's a reminder that even though they may be gone, their story, their impact, and their love will always be a part of us. So, take your time, talk to family members, and think about how you want your loved one to be remembered. There's no right or wrong way to do it—just whatever feels meaningful to you.

A legacy goes beyond preserving memories—it's about keeping the essence of your loved one alive in the hearts of those who knew them and even those who didn't. Be creative and resourceful. If you have children or other relatives who were close to your loved one, involve them in the process. This is an opportunity to create something lasting and meaningful, a tribute that honors their life and brings comfort to the family for generations to come. Whether it's a photo book, a memorial page, or simply sharing stories, creating a legacy is a way to celebrate the life they lived and the love they gave.

Share the Banana LOVE

Tell your friends and family about this book.

Spread the word about the little joys, tips, and insights you've picked up along the way.

And if you really loved it, please consider leaving a five-star review on Amazon.

Your review can help others discover how to bring more joy, humor, and connection to their own caregiving experience.

Plus, who doesn't love a good banana story, right?

Banana Wisdom

"Life's sweeter when you peel away the worries and enjoy the moment."

"Like bananas, the best moments ripen with patience and love."

"When life gets slippery, grab a banana and keep moving forward."

"Peel back the layers of life, and you'll find the sweetest connections."

"In life, you don't need to be perfect, just perfectly ripe for the moment."

"Bananas may bruise, but their sweetness still shines through—just like us."

"Sometimes the simplest pleasures, like a banana, bring the greatest joy."

"Don't let small peels trip you up—every stumble is just part of the journey."

"Life is like a banana—sometimes you slip, but you always get back up."

"No matter how many times you peel back life, there's always sweetness to be found."

"A banana a day reminds us that life's small joys are worth repeating."

"In a world full of chaos, find your banana—a simple joy that never fades."

"Like a bunch of bananas, life is better when shared with the ones you love."

"Peel away expectations and savor the moment, one bite at a time."

ACKNOWLEDGMENT

Dad,

Thank you for all the fun, the laughter, and the little moments that will stay with me forever. You weren't the kind of dad to sit me down and teach life lessons directly, but you had a way of making life enjoyable, of showing me how to find humor in the everyday moments, and how to keep things light. The jokes, the yodeling, the funny stories—it's those moments of joy that I'll always remember.

Even after dementia became a part of our lives, you never lost that spark. You showed me that even when things get tough, there's still room for laughter, for love, and for finding happiness in the small things—like sharing a banana or telling the same story over and over again with just as much excitement each time.

I'm grateful for the times we had, for the smiles, the quirks, and the lessons I didn't even realize I was learning. Thank you for being you and for all the moments—big and small—that made our time together unforgettable.

You gave me life and I was honored to help you live your final years with joy, love, and dignity.

With BIG LOVE,

Bumpsy

Banana Bread Recipe Stories

Once Upon A Time...

1. The Tale of the Classic Banana Bread

Once upon a time, in a cozy little kitchen, three ripe bananas were lounging on the counter, dreaming of their destiny. Little did they know, their grand adventure was about to begin!

Along came a baker, whisk in hand, ready to create something magical. She grabbed the bananas and mashed them with a fork, whispering, "You're going to be stars!"

Into the bowl they went, joined by 1/3 cup of melted butter, like a warm embrace on a chilly morning. The baker then added 3/4 cup of sugar, turning the mixture into a sweet symphony. But the bananas weren't done yet—oh no! An egg, beaten and ready for action, dove into the bowl, followed by one teaspoon of vanilla extract for a touch of elegance.

"Something's missing," thought the baker, and with a wink, she added one teaspoon of baking soda and a tiny pinch of salt to give the bread some lift. Then, 1 1/2 cups of flour gently rained down, turning the batter into a fluffy dream.

With a swift motion, she poured the batter into a greased 9x5-inch loaf pan and into the oven at 350°F (175°C) it went. The bananas were on their final journey, baking for 60-65 minutes until they were golden brown and irresistible.

When the loaf emerged, it cooled just long enough for the baker to slice it open, revealing the most glorious, warm, and soft banana bread. The bananas, now heroes, lived happily ever after... in the bellies of those who devoured them!

2. The Legend of the Banana Nut Bread

In a faraway land (or perhaps just your kitchen), there were three bananas hanging out with a handful of nuts. They were waiting, hoping to join forces in a mighty battle against hunger. One day, their call was answered!

A brave baker grabbed the bananas and mashed them, and with 1/2 cup of melted butter, she turned the mixture into a smooth and buttery concoction. The bananas rejoiced! Soon, 3/4 cup of sugar joined the fun, followed by an egg—beaten but not defeated—and one teaspoon of vanilla extract for some extra charm.

Next came the battle armor: 1 teaspoon of baking soda and a pinch of salt for strength. Then, as if snowflakes were falling from the sky, 1 1/2 cups of flour fluttered into the bowl, giving the mixture substance and heart.

But wait, the bananas needed allies! In marched 1/2 cup of chopped walnuts (or pecans, depending on the kingdom), ready to add their crunch to the mix.

The baker, now fully prepared, poured the batter into a greased loaf pan and sent it off to the oven at 350°F (175°C) for 55-65 minutes. The bananas and nuts braved the heat, emerging victorious as a perfectly baked loaf of banana nut bread.

And as the loaf cooled, the baker knew that the crunchy, nutty goodness inside would satisfy even the hungriest of warriors. Victory— and a delicious snack—was theirs!

3. The Great Chocolate Chip Banana Bread Adventure

In the magical land of Bananaville, three very ripe bananas had one wish: to become something amazing. They had heard stories of chocolate chip banana bread, and it sounded like the dream of a lifetime!

One sunny day, their dream came true. A baker, full of cheer, picked them up and mashed them with love. Into the bowl they went, joined by 1/2 cup of melted butter that made everything smooth as silk. But the magic had just begun!

3/4 cup of sugar danced into the bowl, followed by an egg that was beaten until light and fluffy. The baker sprinkled in 1 teaspoon of vanilla extract to give the bread a little sophistication.

But wait! What's banana bread without a little structure? In came one teaspoon of baking soda and a pinch of salt. And like the final piece of the puzzle, 1 1/2 cups of flour was gently folded into the mix.

Just when the bananas thought they couldn't be happier, the baker reached for something special—3/4 cup of chocolate chips! These sweet morsels tumbled into the batter, turning the simple banana bread into a chocolatey masterpiece.

The baker poured the batter into a greased loaf pan, slid it into the oven, and the bananas embarked on their journey at 350°F (175°C). For 60-65 minutes, they baked, with the chocolate melting into gooey perfection.

When the loaf emerged, the smell of bananas and chocolate filled the air. The baker sliced the loaf, revealing the perfect blend of sweet bananas and melted chocolate. The bananas had reached their ultimate destiny—banana bread with a chocolate twist!

And thus, with full hearts (and stomachs), the baker, the bananas, and the world lived happily ever after... with banana bread in hand, of course!

DAVID'S OTHER BOOKS

Footsteps After the Fall

Dancing with Energy Vampires

Second Mouse Gets the Cheese

What if Today Were the Day?

Who are you fooling?

Egg Nog. Elves. Oy Vey.

Valentines Energy Vampire Detox

Halloween Energy Vampire Blasters

Footsteps after the Fall

DAVID LLOYD STRAUSS

"A falling rock landed on my head and opened my heart." -David L. Strauss

~ A Real Life Experience ~

129

SECOND MOUSE
GETS THE CHEESE

FEELING TRAPPED BY MISTAKES, BAD ADVICE OR INEXPERIENCE?

Upgrade your thinking
Make smarter decisions
Build strong relationships

DAVID LLOYD STRAUSS

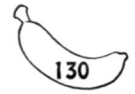

WHAT *if* TODAY *were the* DAY?

a pocket book by
DAVID LLOYD STRAUSS

Who Are YOU Fooling?

David Lloyd Strauss

Egg Nog, Elves & Oy Vey!

Holiday Family Drama Survival Guide

DAVID LLOYD STRAUSS

Footsteps after the Fall

DAVID LLOYD STRAUSS

"A falling rock landed on my head and opened my heart." - David L. Strauss

~ A Real Life Experience ~

VALENTINE'S
ENERGY VAMPIRE DETOX

Break free from toxic relationships. Discover authentic Self Love.

DAVID LLOYD STRAUSS

135

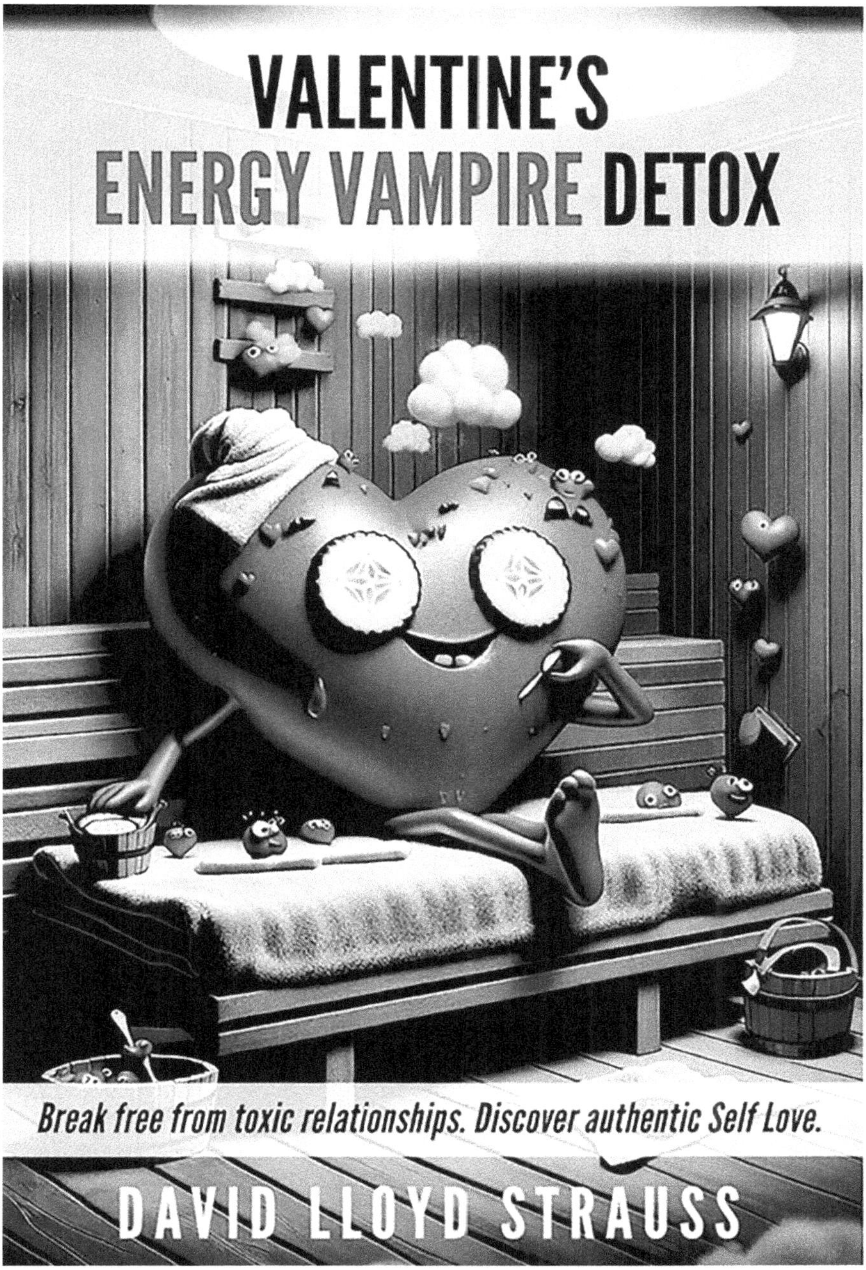

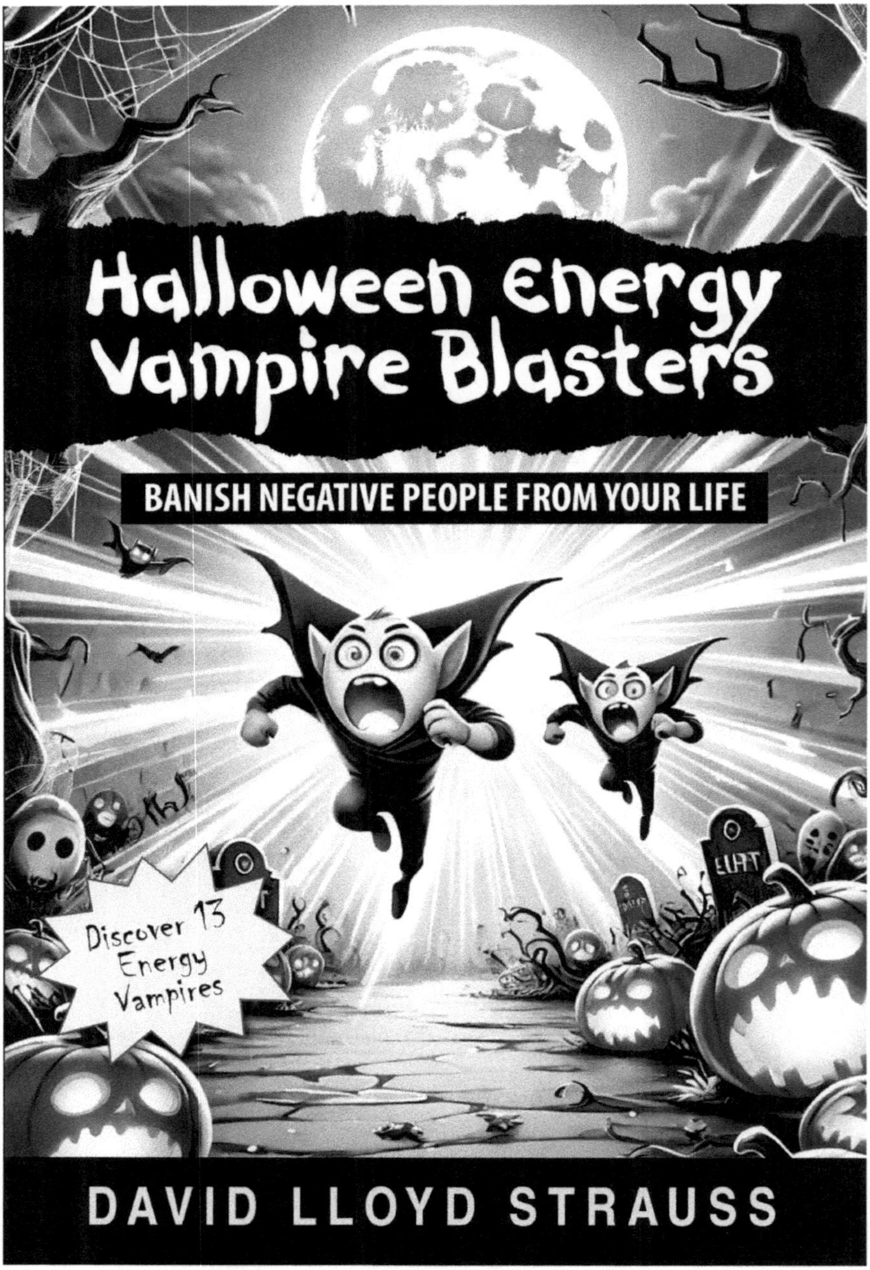

Halloween Energy Vampire Blasters

BANISH NEGATIVE PEOPLE FROM YOUR LIFE

Discover 13 Energy Vampires

DAVID LLOYD STRAUSS

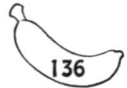

WRITE THAT BOOK ALREADY

Let David Strauss help you write and publish your book!

Author Coaching · Ghost Writing

Editing · Publishing

Done for you OR Done with you!

Go to: DavidStrauss.com

ABOUT THE AUTHOR
DAVID LLOYD STRAUSS

When a falling rock struck David Strauss on the head during a visit to the ancient ruins of Chaco Canyon, New Mexico, his life took an unexpected turn. What began as a near-death experience became a pivotal moment, one that would shape his path and later capture the attention of major affiliate TV networks like ABC, NBC, CBS, FOX, and Success Today. His walk through the desert with an open head injury and concussion redirected the entire trajectory of David's life.

Through years of healing, David uncovered a profound sense of purpose, driven by the desire to make a lasting and meaningful impact on people's lives. This life-changing experience has become the foundation from which he shares transformational messages about self-responsibility, resilience, and growth.

David's journey led him to publish over nine books, each offering insights on personal development, including the Giggle Yoga Philosophy, which embraces lightheartedness as a path to self-discovery, and his concept of Energy Vampire Blasters, teaching others how to release negativity and nurture empowering relationships. With over 20 years of experience inspiring individuals to live with greater purpose, his infectious energy and genuine love for people shine through in his work.

David's passion for self-development and his unique story has made him a sought-after speaker. He was honored to speak at the United Nations HQ for the Global Entrepreneurship Initiative. He continues to create partnerships with individuals and organizations dedicated to uplifting humanity, embodying his commitment to a life lived with purpose, joy, and resilience.

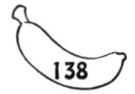

www.ingramcontent.com/pod-product-compliance
Lightning Source LLC
Chambersburg PA
CBHW051208120626
46547CB00013B/1264